Healthy

Presents

Money Basics
For Young Adults

By Don Chambers, CPA, MBA, PFP

For information email: don@healthywealth.com
http://healthywealth.com

For ordering:
http://healthywealth.com
http://amazon.com

ISBN 0-9722071-2-0
ISBN 0-9722071-2-0-978

Contents

Chapter 5 – Insurance 41

Chapter 6 – Spending 44

Chapter 7 - Your Identity & Money 51

Chapter 1 – Introduction

What if you could quickly and easily learn the most important aspects of money matters that you need in life rather than through the school of hard knocks? That is the purpose of this book. I have compiled a quick and easy course on practical money matters I wish I had learned as I was starting out in the world.

It seems obvious that real life money matters should be a required course in both high school and college. Someday I am confident it will be.

As with most things in life it is important to master the fundamentals first. *Money Basics* is an essential primer for dealing with money successfully. People tend to want the more complex information before they have mastered the basics. Take a skill like hitting a baseball. Until you have mastered the basics it is hard to learn how to go with an outside pitch and hit it to the opposite field successfully. Some of you will want to hit a home run before you learn to master hitting to specific locations. Managing money matters is no different. Until you learn to reliably handle the fundamentals trying to accomplish the more complex financial tasks can easily end in disappointment.

What if I could tell you the one most important skill to master about money? I can promise you that if you learn this skill and continue to develop it you will be successful with money for the rest of your life. You will control money it will not control you. Are you interested in developing that skill?

I had 4,500 active clients in my financial planning practice. I retired at age 46. This skill was always present in the clients who were most successful with money. This skill was always lacking in my most financially challenged clients. Simply developing this skill created other positive and successful practices around money all without any more work. I have identified this all important and transforming money fundamental, and a little later in this book I will reveal it to you and help you understand how to learn and develop this skill for yourself.

Knowledge is understanding with increasing distinction. A solid development of the fundamentals of good money management can make all the difference to how you interact with money your entire life. Mastering of the fundamentals of money matters is essential to your long term financial success in life. Even adults will read this book as the school of hard knocks does not guarantee that you will properly master money fundamentals. You must practice the right things to develop good fundamentals.

"I find it fascinating that most people plan their vacations with better care than they plan their lives. Perhaps that is because escape is easier than change."

- Jim Rohn

Chapter 2 - Banking

Purpose of a checking account

Banks provide us with a place to deposit our checks and our cash. We then can write a check, use a debit card, or authorize a charge against our checking account to pay for things. Just about everything you receive and spend goes through your checking account. You pay for your credit card bill from your checking account. The details of your credit card transactions are in your credit card bill.

Filling out a check.

Date:

Today's date. Post dating a check is when you write a future date on a check. Banks will not verify the date on a check so you have no guarantee that post dating a check will keep it from being debited (taken from) your account immediately. (FYI - credited is the opposite of debited and means added to your account).

Pay to the Order of:

To whom you are paying. It is better to write out the full name. Like - Internal Revenue Service, not IRS.

$:

The numbers that represent the payment amount.

_____ Dollars:

Here you must write out the amount of the payment. The bank uses the written description as the amount because it is more difficult to change.

Example #1:

$17.45
"Seventeen 45/100 ———————"
A solid line should be drawn in after the 45/100 (cents) if there is space.

Example #2:

$1,235.11

"One Thousand Two Hundred Thirty-Five 11/100 ——"
The check says "dollars" so you do not have to write it.

Monthly check fees

Many banks offer students a checking program at a reduced monthly fee. Sometimes they require the parent's bank at the same institution in the same state. There is typically no limit on the number of checks you can write a month. Online access to download transactions is usually free. Online Bill Pay usually has a charge. Returned physical checks are now a thing of the past. Copies of the checks are considered legal documents. By using duplicate checks your need for a physical check is reduced further. Duplicate checks will be explained shortly.

Check card / debit card / ATM card

Some banks are now charging students a $1.00 a month fee to have this card and use it for purchases each month. No charge is typically assessed if you just use it to withdraw cash or make deposits at that banks' ATM machines.

Choosing a bank

The most important criteria should be access to ATM machines without paying a fee. You should select a bank that has a good local presence in ATMs, near where you live, where you work, go to school and in your home town.

Most large banks have similar programs for college students.

Using the same bank as your parents can be a convenience especially if you get money regularly every month from your parents. It also helps if you ever need emergency cash.

I recommend having an automatic transfer setup each month from your parents to your account. When you bank at the same bank and do these for the same amount every month on the same date many banks will do these for free.

Bounced check fees.

These can be very expensive and are avoidable. Most banks now

charge $20 to $30 for a bounced check and the store you purchased the goods from may charge you another $20. If a bounced
check results in a late payment on a loan or a credit card payment
it will negatively affect your credit rating. Paying $50 for each
bounced check is an outrageous waste of your precious money.

Paying $50 in bounced check fees for a check totaling $10 is
bad financial management. Think of it as going to your ATM
machine withdrawing $60, buying lunch for $10 and throwing
the other $50 in the trash on purpose.

The tendency is to blame the system. Stop. You know the rules,
you goofed up. Your reaction should be directed at not letting it
happen again.

If you bounce one check a month for two years you would have
wasted around $1,200 on unnecessary bank fees. What could
you do with $1,200? Many of your fellow students will waste
$300 in bank fees in their first year. How much effort should you
put out to save $300 in bank fees? It takes a lot of extra hours in a
side job to earn and keep $300 or especially $1,200 after payroll
and income taxes.

There are two main approaches that work well in avoiding
bounced checks:

Approach 1:
Always keep a positive balance in your account. This works every
time. To do that you need to have a cushion in your account at all
times. This is the best way to manage your account, and yes it
requires discipline. Set $500 as your caution level and $300 as
you're never to go below that amount. Once you hit $500 get
cautious with everything you think about spending and only use
cash until the end of the month. Another way to manage your
account is to keep excellent records. This means posting checks
you have written to your Quicken® or Money® software and regularly going online to update your account.

Approach 2:
Always have overdraft protection available for your checking

account. I will explain overdraft protection next.

Approach 3:
Use approach 1 with approach 2 as a backup. This is the pre-ferred approach.

Overdraft protection
One way to avoid bounced check fees is to have overdraft protection on your checking account that is not maxed out. Banks today prefer to provide overdraft protection through a credit card. Caution - If your credit card is maxed out the over-draft protection will not be there for your checking account.

Overdraft protection is an automatic loan agreement you have set up with your checking account. The bank agrees to loan you money in fixed multiples of $10, $50 or $100. They advance this from a credit card. A cash advance is subject to fees. This is typically $1 or $2 or 2% of the transaction whichever is greater. This is still a lot better than $50 for a bounced check. Even paying 24% interest for a month where you could not repay your credit card is better than $50 in bounced check fees.

Where is the best place to determine if you have available cash left in your checking account? Is it the ATM machine? Is it your online balance? Or your check book running balance? Is it your banking software like Quicken® or Money®?

It is your banking software after doing a download and inputting all your checks that have not yet cleared.

You should payoff your overdraft protection as soon as possible. Your credit card should always have room to absorb any cash advances needed for overdraft protection. Interest and late fees on credit cards really add up so these must be factored in when making sure you have available overdraft protection. Remember overdraft protection is provided in even amounts of $10, $50 or $100 depending on the policy of the plan you are in.

Overdraft protection is there as a backup for when you run a little short at the end of the month. Most students start with a

$500 limit in their overdraft protection plan. The overdraft protection limit you have should be no more than you could payoff in 3 months if you used the entire credit limit for an unexpected emergency. If you find yourself having used up your over draft protection to make an emergency repair to your car, you need to cut back dramatically on all spending until you get your credit card paid off.

Bank account reconciliation

Account reconciliation on your checking account should be done as soon as your bank statement comes in. I do mine within one or two days of getting the statement, and often the same night I get the statement. This may seem like an obsessive compulsive behavior but it is really just a good financial habit. Establishing an attitude of being on top of your money is one of the keys to good money management. Not opening and processing your statement shortly after it comes in is poor financial management.

Financial Success Belief
It is important to reconcile my bank statement to my banking software as soon as the statement comes to my home.

Check register

A check register is a balance tracking device. Traditionally this was kept in with your check book. With the advent of ATMs, auto utility payments, and debit cards it has become much more difficult to keep a manual check register accurate and up to date. For this reason I believe the use of a manual check register is no longer desirable.

Instead, I recommend you download bank activity to your computer no less than once a week and preferably more often. If things are tight do this daily. I recommend you use banking software like Quicken® or Money® to download your bank transactions and input your hand written checks that have not yet cleared.

Where does the money go?

When you use financial software like Quicken® or Money® you

also are asked to categorize each check. For most people everything goes through their checking account so this is a complete record of where your money is being spent. When you take cash out I recommend you simply code this as cash expenses and not try to track where the cash goes.

The most valuable feature of this software is the ability to download all cleared transactions for your checking account and credit card. Yes, I said credit card. With all the fraud today it is a good idea to review all your credit card activity regularly as well.

Some banks have their own check book software. I do not recommend this software. I prefer Quicken® as it works with all other banks and all other credit cards.

There is no important difference between Quicken® and Money®. The latest versions do not provide any important features needed by students. It is reasonable to assume you can stay with your initial purchase for three or so years with no loss in functionality. Some new computer purchases come with Quicken® or Money® included in the software bundle.

There are three types of data importation from banks into Quicken® or Money®. Most big banks provide direct importation into Quicken® and Money®. Some credit unions and small banks do not allow you to directly import their data into Quicken® and Money®. You then have an extra step or two to go through to get the data. I find this extra step slows me down and discourages me from wanting to update my data. Quicken.com lists the banks and credit unions that allow direct download.

Electronic bill payment

The simplest form of electronic bill payment is to authorize your utility payments to automatically come out of your checking account each month. You can do this either when you first establish service or anytime later. If you share an apartment you may not want to do this.

Banks and Quicken offer a bill payment service. Quicken's current fees are $9.95 for the first 20 payments, and $2.49 for each additional set of payments. Wells Fargo Bank (typical large bank) fees for Bill Pay are considerably lower at $6.95 a month for the first 25 payments and each additional payment costs $0.40.

The breakeven (postage costs) on Wells Fargo's bill pay is 19 checks a month. So if you are sending out 12 checks a month the actual cost of this service is only $0.37 x 5 = $1.85 a month.

The Quicken® plan never breaks even with the out of pocket postage costs. 20 bills at $0.37 each only equals $7.40, thus it always costs you at least $2.59 a month for the service. Their $2.49 charge for one to five more checks is fairly costly. In general Quicken Bill Pay service is much more costly than a typical bank's Bill Pay service today.

The advantage of Quicken Bill Pay is that if you switch banks you do not have to set up the addresses and payees again. That is a small hassle for such a large cost difference.

There is another form of electronic bill payment you should know about. It is useful when you travel a lot. It can be helpful when you want to automate the receipt and payment of your bills. There are bill paying services like http://www.paytrust.com that receive your bills and pay them according to preestablished rules you setup. All mail goes to them, they scan it and pay according to rules you set up. All communications are done via email. Unmatched bills and bills that are over your pre-authorized limit are brought to your immediate attention by email. All payments are notified to you by email.

If you are responsible for paying the bills in your household and you travel for more than a few days at a time, or on a regular basis then services like http://www.paytrust.com can be a valuable tool. Even if all you want is reliability in the auto payment of regular bills then this kind of a service is worth using instead of electronic bill pay with a bank or Quicken®.

This service currently costs $10.95 a month for the first 30 transactions (works out to be about 18 bills paid) and then $0.50 a transaction. A transaction is both the paper coming in and the check going out, no charge is levied for a bill received electronically. The cost for this service works out to around $5.00 a month when you take away typical savings in stamps.

With this service you will have an online record (PDF documents) of all your bills and payments. You can access your records online 24/7 from anywhere. It is possible to make payments to anyone in the United States while on the road without having your check book, an envelope or a stamp.

Using automatic payment systems to pay your regular bills is a good idea. It keeps your bills paid on time and this helps protect your credit rating. You still must make sure you have a sufficient balance at all times in your checking account to cover these automatic payments.

Electronic bill paying services are a convenience rather than a necessity. I personally do not mind spending the $5 net a month to make my life easier and more timely around bill receipt and paying. I travel a lot, so this service works very well for me.

If this service saved you one late fee or one turnoff and reconnect fee a year it pays for itself and makes your life easier in the process. This is an individual choice. As a student you may find saving $5.00 a month at 18 bills paid, or $9.50 at only 6 bills paid a month, too costly for you.

If you are going to sign up for a Bill Pay service at an additional $6 a month then consider this service as it is more for about the same price as Bill Pay. If you take a job that requires you to travel, then remember that this kind of service makes paying your bills more reliable and saves you time.

Account balance

Keep an accurate ongoing account balance. This simple act is a good measure of how responsible you are with your money. Your choices are the online software provided by your bank, Quicken® or Money® software you install on your computer. With Quicken® and Money® software you first download your transactions and then manually input any new checks you have written but have not cleared. If you mailed a deposit in you may need to input it as an addition to the account manually. The balance showing at the bottom is your "book" balance, and represents what you have available.

This way of balancing your account is quite a bit different than what your parents were taught, but a more practical adaptation to the modern world.

One feature I like about Quicken® or Money® software is the ability to look back at when in the month auto payments are taken from your account. You can also easily see the amount. You can sort by payee by a click of a button, or by amount to find things easily. You will like this kind of time saving lookup feature. Answering questions and solving problems takes more time, so I like tools that make these tasks easier.

When you use your ATM card these transactions are available on the banks records either immediately or the next business day.

Credit card charges usually take a few days to post. There are two dates on your credit card statements, the transaction date and the posted date. This is because of the banking procedures currently required to process credit card charges.

Duplicate checks

I recommend you use duplicate checks. When you write a check and a carbonless copy of that check remains in your check book, this is called a duplicate check. Duplicate checks cost a little more. I find they are worth it, even when you only need to utilize it once a year.

Ordering checks

Checks purchased from your bank can cost twice as much as checks ordered from check printing companies. I personally use the Costco check printing service. It costs me around $8.50 U.S. today for 200 duplicate checks, and this includes the shipping charges. I usually get my checks about 10 days after they are ordered. Online check printing companies vary in their charges. These services generally are safe and reliable. Never let new blank checks sit in your unlocked mail box.

Auto deposit

Auto deposit your payroll check into your checking account, even for part time work. This saves time, is more convenient and can eliminate your monthly checking account fee. Some people have said they prefer getting a check in their hand. I disagree. There are only two reasons to not auto deposit a pay check for full or part time work. The first is you do not have a checking account, but that should be changed. Second, your employer does not provide this service yet.

Auto deposits go straight to your account the day they are paid. You will get a printed deposit summary from your employer showing your gross pay, deductions and the net pay.

Auto payments

Auto payments for utilities and loan payments are a good thing; you have to pay these anyway. These happen at the same time each month and you typically get your mailed statement a week or so ahead of the deduction so you know what is going to be taken out of your account.

ATM Access fees

Avoid paying fees at ATM machines to get access to your cash. If you have to pay a fee then learn what machines charge the least.

Selecting a bank that has ATMs readily available in the areas you frequent is important. If you pay a $2 access fee from another bank your bank is likely to also charge you $1. If you take $40 out this way you just paid an 8% cash access fee! I hate getting ripped off like that. Would you agree to pay a $3 fee every month to pay a $40 phone bill by credit card rather than by check? So why throw away $3 at the ATM to get $40 in cash?

Chapter 3 – Credit Cards

Let's talk about the most common and costly financial mistake made by young adults with money - Credit Cards. Make no mistake credit cards can get you in some serious financial trouble before you know it. It can take years, many years in fact to get yourself out of a few months of credit card mistakes.

It may make you temporarily feel good to make an impulse purchase or exercise that credit line. The hang over for excessive credit card use (when your balance is not paid off in full for at least 9 months of the year) is far worse than you can imagine until you experience it. What young adults report about this experience is that they feel angry and dismayed at the predicament they find themselves in. The fees and interest added on by the credit card companies are abusive. It is hard to imagine these fees could be legal. There are laws that limit the interest rate and the fees, but they allow the credit card companies to make an awful lot of money from people who do not manage their credit very well.

Let's explore credit cards and how they work and how you can use them properly.

Credit card companies make the most profit from people who have a balance on their card at the end of the billing period. They make a smaller profit from the store where you made your purchase.

When you go to a store and use a credit card, that store has to pay a fee of around 1.2% to 6% of the transaction to the credit card company for processing the transaction.

The credit card companies make big profits off credit card users who do not pay their account balances off in full every month. The interest rate and late payment penalties make them staggering profits.

The next story is real and was shared with me. Managing credit and credit cards is a learned skill, and it starts with a realistic and healthy respect for the pain and cost of not paying off your balance in full every month.

Credit card story:

All through my adolescent and teenage years all I wanted to be was 18. At 18 you are considered an adult by society.

On my 18th birthday, I did two very adult things. I applied for two credit cards, and purchased my first lottery ticket. I applied for a Discover card and a Visa through Capital One. The Discover card people had a table set up at my school, conveniently close to Christmas time. My Capital One card was obtained through an online application, and after some thoughtful consideration, I decided on the beach scene for my "free personalized card design".

I was approved for both cards immediately. I was just 18 years old I had no credit thus far. My Discover card came in a shiny black envelope, and I couldn't have been more excited. How grown up of me to have my own credit card, something I had been looking forward to having since I was about 12 and learned what they were. When I saw the credit limit on my shiny new black card was $1,000 my jaw almost dropped to the ground. Surely there had to be a mistake somewhere. I honestly did not think that I would have qualified for anything more than $500 at the most. Eagerly, I called the 800 number to activate my card, excited to pay with plastic as soon as possible.

My Capital One card came about two days later, and when I applied for that card, I knew my limit would he about $300 - $500. It was $300. But it was such a pretty beach scene. Naively, I thought it was the prettiest thing in my wallet.

I made an empty promise to myself that I would use the cards for emergencies only, and I would not allow my spending to get out of control. But of course it did.

In the first three months I only bought a few things at the mall, some lunches for my friends and a couple of tanks of gas. In all of my spending, I honestly did not think that I would have a problem paying the minimum balance every month. And then the first bills came. Opening them with a somewhat rapid heart beat I saw how much I owed on my Discover card, which was better than I expected, only $75. Then I opened the Capital One statement, the minimum payment was $95. I wrote two checks, sent them in, and that was that. I was proud of my responsibility and what I thought was my savvy money handling.

Spending on my cards became easier. My minimum payment got higher and my available balance got lower. The first payments were the only ones I ever made myself. Looking back on the whole experience, I guess that I thought, or rather wished, that somehow the balances would just disappear, and I wouldn't have to be bothered with paying my cards off. I was desperate to fix the mess I had made. I did not know where to start, and I was scared to ask my family for help. Both of my cards were eventually maxed out in about a six month period from when I initially got them. I did not have enough money to get my balances under control.

My statements were sent to my dad's house and one day he opened my Discover card statement, which was actually a final notice to make a minimum payment of $375. He immediately called me and said we had to find a solution to this, and so we did. He started making my monthly payments, and the Discover card was paid off in about two years. We then cut it up into little pieces.

My Capital One card now had a balance of about $500 and $200 of that was interest and late fees. It was charged off by Capital One, and sent to a collection agency. Once the collection agency contacted me, I knew it was absolutely necessary to pay it off. So I sent the collection agency $150 for two months. After selling my car I sent them a cashier's check for the balance. I also cut this card into little pieces once it was paid off.

As a result of my irresponsible credit behavior, I have a very poor credit report, and I am always asked to make a deposit of at least $200 when signing up for any service.

For the last two years I have taken it very seriously that I cannot and will not apply for any credit cards until I have a career, not just a part time job. I am not at a place in my life right now where making monthly payments on a credit card is something respon- sible, mature or financially reasonable.

I have also eliminated the use of my debit card for quite some time now, and only pay for things in cash or checks. I know that a check card takes money straight out of my checking account, but on more than one occasion, I have used it like a credit card, and have overdrawn myself, which is a completely wasteful thing to do.

Now I am less likely to find myself in money trouble with the fear of being overdrawn on my checking account, or bouncing a check, and so far so good. I only spend what I have, and I have found that I can live beneath my means and still have a good time.

While I would love to establish my name with good credit, I know that I am still young, and I will have time for that. In the meantime I pay my bills on time and am still able to save money every month just in case of an emergency, a real emergency, not a retail crisis. I am almost thankful that I learned about credit the hard way, because I realize now how important credit is.

Credit card interest rates:
Credit card interest rates fall into four basic categories. These categories are a convenient way to categorize what is generally offered today.

1. 7% to 14% teaser rate that lasts for the first 6 months or until you are late on a payment.
2. 14% to 18% never late and always paid in full rate.
3. 18% to 22% never late, but at least the minimum is always paid.
4. 22% to 29% once late on a minimum payment.

Credit card geometric progression example:
Suppose at age 20 you owe $10,000 on your credit card and you are being charged 18% a year in interest. You agree never to

charge anything on this credit card again but decide to take out one new card to make the minimum payment due on the $10,000 balance. How big will your two credit card balances grow in the future?

At age 30 you would now owe $60,000 between the two credit cards. At age 40 you would now owe $356,000 between the two credit cards. At age 50 you would now owe $2,000,000 between the two credit cards. At age 60 you would now owe $12,700,000 between the two credit cards.

This is why you get so many credit card offers in the mail each month. This is a great way for banks and credit card companies to make a lot of money off people who have not learned the importance of keeping their credit cards paid off.

The facts are that most young adults in college or early on in their career have substantial credit card balances today. It is not uncommon for a young adult to owe $10,000 in total to several credit card companies by the time they graduate.

Building credit with your credit card

Did you know that a credit card with late fees will hurt your credit and could block you from your dreams? It is sad but true! It takes a lot of effort to manage your responsibility to always pay your credit card on time.

A lot of young adults are told they need a credit card to establish credit. This is true, but they are not told that even one late payment will damage your credit rating for seven years. In aggregate credit cards can do far more damage to your credit than they help.

If you let your credit cards build up to where you are having difficulty making payments you can be separated from any new credit cards, auto loans, and more. It can put a serious barrier between you and your dreams for many years. An unfavorable credit reporting can stay on your credit report for seven years.

Seven years is also a typical amount of time it takes someone who finally realized they have credit card debt problems to get their credit card debt paid off.

Did you know that a bad credit report can do more than keep you from being able to borrow? It is sad but true, and often learned the hard way.

Many employers today will perform a credit check on a potential employee as part of the hiring process. A potential employee who does not manage their own finances is not a good prospect to deal with the businesses finances. Everything else being equal, would you rather hire an employee with a good credit rating or one with a poor credit rating? Exactly, a bad credit rating can come between you and your dreams.

Let's say you go on a spring break and meet this really exciting and impressive potential partner. As you get to know each other you let on about your credit problems. If that other person holds a high value to managing his or her financial affairs and you do not, what do you think that does to your desirability?

Let's flip things around and say that you are the one with the good credit management skills and you meet this wonderful and interesting person but they have a dark side around credit management. How sure are you about how much of the iceberg you are seeing? What doubts and concerns does this raise for you? Are you compromising your standards in ways that could come back to haunt you? Don't most couples argue most about money? Are you basically incompatible in your values around spending and debt?

All too often those with maxed out credit cards will state they had no idea how letting their credit card balances get a little out of control could hurt their self esteem so much and cut them off from their dreams for so long.

Avoiding this kind of a setback and handicap is all the reason you need to avoid credit card debt problems. Having to put your goals on hold for seven years due to a few months of financial indiscretion is too heavy a price to pay. Don't let that happen to you!

It is better to struggle a little today than struggle your way out of debt and bad credit, possibly for most of your adult life.

The three most common credit card mistakes

1. ***Failure to have and use a credit card strategy*** (rules for credit card use). Waiting to see if you can manage credit cards before setting up a discipline is a prescription for the credit card companies to earn excessive fees and penalties from you.

2. ***Being disorganized in paying your bills.*** This will certainly lead you to the land of excessive credit card and banking fees. Some people take their entire life to learn this lesson. A years worth of careless banking can easily amount to a week's vacation lost. Would you rather be working to go on vacation, or working to pay for your banker to go on vacation? Make it a rule to mail your bills 7 days before the due date. Set your utility bills up for automatic payment from your checking account.

3. ***Paying the Minimum Payment.*** This is your final warning sign of an impending financial crisis. The earlier you respond to this warning and get this debt paid off the sooner you will have a financial life. If you fail to heed this warning it will take you a lot longer and cost you a lot more in lost lifestyle to get out of your financial mess.

Rules for dealing with credit cards

Let me outline some rules for dealing with credit cards.

♦   You should always pay your account in full each month.
♦   If you have a balance that is unpaid on your credit card it should be for no more than three months a year.
♦   If for any reason you have a balance of three or more months a year unpaid on your credit card you have a debt management problem!
♦   How many credit cards do you need? Answer - one.
♦   What is the best card to have? Answer - either a Visa or MasterCard.
♦   What is the best program to enroll in? Answer - When you are young you should have a card that does not have

annual fees. Forget credit cards with airline benefits; the annual fee you pay for this privilege ends up costing more than you get. Surprised? Just review the numbers in the explanation that follows.

Credit cards that offer cash back work. That is why they are rare today.

Airline miles and similar programs encourage over-spending by using the mileage accumulation as an incentive to charge more on the credit card than you would otherwise.

The value of an airline ticket you would receive in ex-change for 25,000 miles today is around $350. It cost you around $25,000 in charges to earn the miles for a free trip. All cards that offer airline miles charge annual fees for the miles. These fees vary from $40 to $80 a year. At $60 a year in fees you breakeven if you take 6 years to earn the miles. To earn 25,000 miles to get a so called "free ticket" in 6 years you must charge $400 a month in credit card charges to break even.

This is assuming everything works out and you purchase the ticket as soon as you have 25,000 miles or points. Lots of things can make this worse and nothing can make it better. The airlines are in financial trouble con-stantly these days so the free seats are harder and harder to get. To get a free ticket to Hawaii you must book more than 6 months in advance in most cases.

If you want to go to Hawaii and you are booking only a month ahead and you want to use miles, they will do it for 65,000 miles, and we are still talking about an economy seat.

♦ What about Sears, Nordstrom, and other specialty cards? These are not a good idea even in the rare case where they do not charge you annual fees. Besides the high rate of interest on balances due, they encourage overspending at that store and they know it. I was standing in line at Victoria's Secret the day before Valentines Day and two young ladies were in line in front of me. One said to the other "I sent in an application for a Victoria Secret credit card but I hope they do not approve me because I would limit it out right away". Something is wrong when you hold yourself as being helpless in credit card management.

♦ Debit cards (bank cards, ATM cards) are a good alternative to credit cards. These cards take the money straight out of your checking account. You are not able to make a charge unless you have the cash to pay for what you are buying now. For most young adults it is better to primarily use a debit card and save the credit card for emergencies and for items your parents will be reimbursing.

♦ If you have a credit card problem today - how do you solve it? Stop using the credit cards and switch to using a debit card. Work out a plan to payoff your credit card balances. This is your most expensive debt. Do a little celebration when each one is paid off. Payoff the smallest accounts faster to get the reinforcement of making progress. Switch over to a low interest rate credit card to help you reduce your interest cost if you still have good enough credit to get a low interest card.

ATM vs. credit cards

Credit cards are issued by banks or financial institutions who are extending you credit. You are billed once a month for charges you make and you have 20 to 25 days from the cutoff date to make your payment. When you use a credit card you sign for the purchase.

An ATM card / Debit Card / Bank Card may have the Visa or MasterCard® logo but it usually has the words "check card" or "debit card". These are also issued by a bank or financial institution. However the main difference is the payment is immediately and automatically deducted from the checking account connected to that card. No credit (time to pay) is associated with the use of this card. You will be asked to input your PIN number when making a purchase with an ATM card / debit card / bank card.

Credit cards charge the store where you use the card a percentage of the transaction, typically between 1.2 percent to 6 percent, plus a fixed fee of around $0.25 a transaction.

Debit cards charge the store typically a fixed fee of $0.10 to $0.30 per transaction. Debit cards are in effect a paperless check.

With a credit card purchase you do not have to pay for the purchase until the billing due date of the next statement. You also have the option to not pay your balance due in full if you pay interest on the outstanding balance.

Credit cards have balance limits. Limits start as low as $300 and go to around $1,500 for a student. For your first credit card a limit of $500 is appropriate.

Borrowing money to live on before you have a permanent job is not a good idea, nor is it a good financial practice. Credit card companies will automatically increase your limit. You can ask them to reduce the limit back to where it was.

College credit cards:

The first day you start college you will find table after table on campus offering to sign you up for credit cards. They will offer you free t-shirts, bags and other promotional items to get you to sign-up. It is not hard to get started with a credit card. It is like offering free cigarettes, they just want to get you hooked.

The main types of credit cards are Visa, MasterCard®, American Express, Discover, and store specific cards (which are Visa or MasterCard).

A college credit card is a credit card with easier qualifications and a lower initial credit limit. Credit card companies liberalize the rules for college students because they know parents are likely to bail them out and they often carry balances earning them a high rate of interest for many years.

Unauthorized charges on credit cards:

As long as you report the loss or unauthorized use of your card on a timely basis you usually are not responsible for these charges. For this reason it is a good idea, when you travel, to have a list of your credit cards at home with your parents. I travel with this list in a password protected file, or if I am going overseas I copy both sides of all the items in my wallet and my passport and leave that with my mom, just in case I need these faxed to me.

"Real success comes when you realize that the mere tokens of success have little meaning. Real success comes when you can be who you are."

- Ralph Marston

Chapter 4 - Cars

Lets examine one of the more desired and expensive aspects of a young adult's life - cars.

To start let me ask you a few questions to find out how you feel about cars and what you think is important about a car.

- Do you think gas mileage matters? If so how important is it in your decision? Will it matter more when you are paying for all your own gas?
- Do you think that a luxury car is important? If you said yes - why?
- Do you think that if you drive a low cost car like a Hyundai this will reflect poorly on you?
- Do you think owning the "in car" will bring you happiness?

Choosing a car

Most people start with a practical approach to choosing a car and then degenerate their decision to emotion based criteria. You might ask yourself questions like:

- What utility do I need from a car?
- Do I need a lot of cargo space and how often will I need it?
- Do I need 4 doors?
- Do I have a long commute and what do I need to make that work? Automatic, good stereo, low road noise, good driver's seat?
- Do I need good snow traction? Front wheel drive, all wheel drive and what kind of tires?
- What kind of city gas mileage rating do I need?
- What cars in the class I am considering are recommended by consumer reports?
- What cars in the class I am considering have the least repair and maintenance problems?
- How often do I really need the extra space of an SUV more than a few times a year?

These are all good questions and help pin point from a utility basis what kind of transportation needs you really have. Often this decision making takes a back seat to the emotional decisions – like:

- What kind of cars do I like as I drive?
- What color of car do I like?
- What cars have the best paint jobs?
- What is hot right now?
- What kind of car do my friends have that I like?
- I must have a car that declares my uniqueness?
- A convertible would be a good choice don't you think?
- I think I would look good in a jeep don't you?

Too often the decision on what car you want to buy is first generated by what you like as you drive around. This typically is based on what your friends and peer group like. It is also based in large part by your ego and what it says about you if you drive such and such a car, truck or SUV. The practical side of the car buying decision gets far too little importance. With this understanding you can see the merit in a rules based process for buying a car to save you from your ego based decision process.

Automobile guidelines (high school / college):

- Your first car in high school is a learning experience. The reality is this car will be scratched, dinged and dented. Soda and fast food will be spilled everywhere. By graduation the carpets will be home to colonies of microscopic creatures multiplying and thriving. This car will be driven hard and abused.

- Your first car should have at least two airbags.

- There are two ways to go with your first car in high school. Option 1, you buy a car for just high school and then a better car for college. Option 2, buy a car in high school that you keep through college. If it is a car you will keep through college your first car should be less than five years old and have less than 60,000 miles.

- Your first car should NOT be an off road dirt eating monster truck.

- This car should be appropriate for high school students, or someone with a part time job. This is a tough one I know. All my kids went nuts over this issue. They all wanted outrageous statements of status. They each fought hard to get that status given to them. This is the wrong way to go for lots of reasons. I know this is not what you want to hear, and most of you will strongly disagree with me now, but by your third year of college you will agree with me. Trust me, you are making a big mistake if you get a status symbol of a car at this stage in life. If your parents let you get away with this they are making a mistake. I know I made it.

It really does matter that you get an age and income appropriate car. Right now you are a part time employees living off welfare (your parents).

A friend and her husband each have a new Mercedes. There is nothing wrong with that, these are great luxury cars. The problem is both are leased so they can afford a car in this price range. These cars have much higher insurance costs, higher maintenance costs and their gas mileage is not impressive. They complain about their lack of money for things yet each time they get a new car it gets more expensive.

The problem occurs when the total car costs are high in relation to your income. This adds stress that could be eliminated from your life. If you have money stress, cutting back on your car costs is a good thing to do. Many people will buy far more car than is needed or they should be buying. This is a very common financial mistake. The problem starts innocently enough when in high school. If your beliefs do not change your car buying behavior never changes.

Does the car you drive make you more successful?

- Your car should not be your mom's used family BMW sedan or any other high end hand me down. If it is a reliable older Toyota Camry sedan then a hand me down is a possibility.

- Good gas mileage is important. Much more important than you know now. I recommend a city rating as high as you can get. Hybrids are fabulous; anything with a 30+ mpg city rating will end up being something you really appreciate when you are on a tight budget outside of the home.

- Insurance costs are an important consideration. I recommend you not get a car whose insurance cost is more than 25% higher than a similar year Honda Accord LX. Ask your parents' insurance agent to fax you both quotes. If you end up being stuck with this car after high school and have to provide your own insurance, this rule will really matter. I have seen this happen to lots of young adults, and it can happen to you.

Getting a good deal on a used car:

- According to Automotive Lease Guide a new car or truck loses 38% of its sticker value after 12 months. This is a good reason to buy a lightly used car. Over three years the average car is projected to lose 56% of its sticker value. If you can find a good used car with 12 to 24 months use you can get an outstanding value for your money. Οφ χουρσε ϖερψ φεω χαρσ αχτυαλλψ σελλ φορ τηειρ στιχκερ πριχε σο τηισ στατιστιχ ισ οϖερ ιν–φλατεδ.

- Today you can lookup on the Internet the value of any car you are considering to buy. Kelly Blue Book is a highly regarded free site for this information. They can be found online at http://kbb.com.

They give you three different prices for used cars. I find only the "trade in value" to be reliable. This is sometimes called "low Blue Book Value". The "retail value" is supposedly what a car dealer will sell you this car for. The "Private

Party Value" is supposedly what a private party price would be. I find cars actually sell in a private party deal for less than they tell you. Car dealers and private sellers can and should be bargained with, as they will often settle for much less than the asking price.

A highly sought after model may cost $1,000 or $1,500 over low Blue Book. Most cars sell for a few hundred dollars over low Blue Book. A car with issues will sell slowly and for something under low Blue Book.

♦   Always get a used car checked by a mechanic before you buy. If you do not have a regular mechanic then take it to the dealer, you at least know they will not be working with the seller. If the problems are more than minor then renegotiate with the seller based on these new findings. Don't expect to get the seller to pay for 100% of what you find if you already got a good price, but you can start your negotiations there.

♦   The more popular a model is the more competitive it will be to obtain that car. Savvy used car buyers know what day and time the new auto traders come out and get their copy right away.

It is a requirement to know the Kelly blue book trade-in value of any year make and model you are considering. This is the price you should be negotiating from. I recommend you make a written list of all cars that catch your interest as you read the ads. This quick summary helps you understand prices and value much faster than just juggling this input in your head.

♦   Paying for the car. Sellers want to be paid in full. If you are financing the car have everything ready to go. Sellers want a deal to close in a few days.

♦   On a used car loan get a three or four year repayment term. Five or seven years is just too long on a used car. Credit Unions typically have the best used car loan rates.

Ask your parents if they are a member of a credit union. If so, they can sign you up.

♦ Do not buy the last year of a model before a major change. You will often see a substantial cost savings but this last year before a major model change is difficult to resell.

Tips on buying a new car:

♦ You must know the "Dealer Invoice" price of a car before beginning the negotiation part of buying. There are two prices for a new car "MSRP" (Manufacturers Suggested Retail Price) and "Dealer Invoice". When you look at the window sticker on a car it shows the MSRP price.

♦ Most new cars sell for dealer invoice plus several hundred dollars before considering any manufacturers rebates. Premium and hot models often sell close to MSRP and occasionally for a short time at a premium above MSRP.

♦ When buying from a dealer expect the process to take you three hours of negotiating and be emotionally gut wrench-ing. This is just how the game is played today for buying most cars in America. To find out what price you should be paying for a new car I recommend knowing the Kelly Blue Book Dealer Invoice price. It is also worth paying $15 for a Consumer Report's new car buying service to know more about local selling prices. It is valuable to know what the target premium is today for your car in your marketplace. Another website that can help you do this is http:// Edmunds.com.

♦ Year end model closeouts are often not the best buy. It often pays to buy the newer model. The exception would be when the model did not change much, you are going to keep the car for a long time and the savings are substan-tial.

♦ If there is a significant model change do not buy the old year model no matter how much discount they give.

How much car can you afford?

When I was growing up my grandfather, Harold Hutton, loved cars and he owned a Ferrari. It was a 1966 Ferrari 500 Superfast. There were only six of these made. It would go 185 miles an hour. First gear went to 60 miles an hour, second gear went to 90, and there were 6 gears. My grandfather proudly declared that some-day this car would be mine.

My grandfather died while I was finishing college. At the time I could not afford the insurance on this car, nor could I afford to rent a house with a garage. I could not afford to tune this car. I could not afford the eight layers of paint this car required every ten years. So my grandmother put the car into her garage and stored it. Even when I bought my first house, with a garage, at age 28 I still could not afford the insurance or the upkeep for this car. I still dreamed of owning this car and driving it on the country roads around Santa Barbara where I lived at the time on the weekend, the way a Ferrari wants to be driven.

A few years later my grandmother decided to sell the Ferrari without talking to me about it. I had mixed emotions. I was greatly disappointed, and saddened she had not discussed this with me. On the other hand I felt relieved. Now many years later I am sad about it, but know it was right then.

My biggest fear at the time was that its presence in my garage would place a lot of pressure on me to give up doing other things I loved doing at the time. I was not willing to trade my golf and surfing time for this car. I did not want to trade my vacations every two years to Maui for this car. I really wanted this car; it was just going to be a while until my financial life could afford the owner-ship of such a car.

This Ferrari may be a bit of an extreme case, but it does represent the same choices we each have to make about cars. It is also a fact that cars are expensive. The culture in much of the modern world today encourages the ownership of a more expensive car as a way to demonstrate we are successful to ourselves and to others. The flip side is the more expensive a car you buy the less you can do other things.

How much car is prudent to purchase?

This is a rough guide and conservative enough to leave room for other things like vacations and recreation. Your trade-off between a car and your other things is a personal choice.

Annual Income	Price of Car
$ 20,000	$12,000
$ 30,000	$15,000
$ 40,000	$18,000
$ 50,000	$21,000
$ 60,000	$24,000
$ 70,000	$26,000
$ 80,000	$29,000
$ 90,000	$31,000
$100,000	$33,000

Parents buying your car?

Does it matter what the price is of your car if your parents buy it for you? Yes!

Do you know anyone whose parents bought him or her a new $40,000+ car or SUV in high school or as they went off to college?

- Do you think they will turn out better or worse for receiving this car as a gift?
- How many of these students took really good care of this car?
- How many of these students believe their parents will bail them out of whatever financial mess they get into?
- How many of these students do you think will keep buying cars that are more expensive than they should be because of this experience?
- Do you think it is a good idea for parents to buy expensive new cars for their college or high school age students?
- Do you think that students would be better off driving cars that are economical and safe, rather than expensive?

What is the best way to finance a car?

♦ Credit Unions typically have the lowest interest rates for car loans.

♦ Bank loans are moderate in price, but still very reasonable.

♦ Auto dealer loans are the most convenient, but typically the most expensive.

♦ It is best to first narrow down the car price range you are interested in and then get a financing application in at your bank or credit union.

Should you lease or buy your next car?

Leasing has a lower monthly cash outflow requirement, but almost always costs more than buying. Leasing also encourages you to buy more car than you should. Leasing can cost more because:

♦ Interest rates are usually higher in a lease agreement because they are hidden from you in a lease.

♦ The purchase price you pay is typically higher with a lease as all the focus is on the monthly payment amount.

♦ Lease deals hide costs and thus the dealers will stick you with costs you would avoid or negotiate away in a purchase.

♦ Sales tax payments are higher in a lease program than with a purchase, as you pay sales tax on the interest as well.

How long should you keep a car?

♦ Depends on where you live. Salted roads wear out cars sooner.

♦ Warm climates, 7-12 years is target for a new car to get maximum value.

♦ Snowy climates, 6-10 years is target for a new car to get maximum value.

♦ The longer you keep a car typically the lower your total ownership cost. Once a car has over 60,000 miles its maintenance costs usually start to rise.

Best options for buying a used car?

♦ Many new cars have recently been sold on a two year

lease. These can be good buys. You will most likely be
buying from a dealer. Avoid the extended warranty offer.

- Lookup the Kelly Blue Book trade-in value on the Internet
  before buying. Telling the dealer you are willing to pay $150
  over low blue book and let them know you know the low
  blue book value for the car.
- Only buy a car that consumer reports rate as recommended. Certain manufacturers, like Toyota and Honda,
  have nearly all their cars on the recommended list.
- Do not buy a used car whose repair rating is at or below
  average.
- Do not buy a used car on the Internet. This is where the
  lemons cars and fraudulent sellers go. I bought two cars
  this way, and had both checked first. Both ended up with
  hidden problems. I can say with experience this is a bad
  idea. If you buy this way your chances of getting a problem
  car is much higher than normal.

Auto maintenance

- Have the oil changed as recommended by manufacturer,
  typically every 5,000 to 10,000 miles. The 3,000 mile oil
  change promoted by Jiffy Lube and the other oil change
  companies is not what most car manufacturers recommend. That said changing your oil and oil filter on time is
  the most important thing you can do to assure a long life
  for your car.
- Fix what sounds bad right away.
- Find an honest mechanic. Ask your friends who they use
  and ask if they would recommend that mechanic. Also ask
  them how long they have used the mechanic.

What Grade of Gasoline?

- Modern engine controls automatically adjust cars to run
  perfectly, with no knocking (value grinding) or risk of damage, on lower octane regular gas. Even when the manufacturer recommends 91 octane your car may run fine on 87
  octane. Try the lower octane and if during acceleration your
  car engine does not knock (value pinging) you probably do
  not need to buy the higher octane gas. Also contrary to

popular misconception higher octane gas does not improve gas mileage.

"Our best friends and our worst enemies are our thoughts. A thought can do us more good than a doctor or banker or a faithful friend. It can also do us more harm than a brick."

- Dr. Frank Crane

Chapter 5 – Insurance

Auto insurance

Auto insurance is necessary to protect you from liability (collision) and loss of your vehicle from an accident (comprehensive).

- Your best deal is usually to stay on your parent's policy for as long as you are allowed.
- When you purchase your own insurance you need to do some work to figure out the best deal. Different insurance companies treat younger drivers differently.
- The rate of change in insurance premiums today is very fast, so do not assume the same company from three years ago will be the best today.
- It is important to keep a clean driving record, no more than one ticket in the last three years.
- It is a fact of life that cops focus on young drivers.
- A DUI is one of the biggest mistakes you can make; it will cost you for up to seven years in car insurance premiums.
- Once you reach 25 years of age your car insurance rates usually drop significantly.

Rental car auto insurance

Most rental car companies will not rent to anyone under 21. Call ahead and verify. Generally your auto insurance covers you for a rental car unless you have restricted coverage. If you are on your parent's policy you may have a restricted policy. Before going on a trip where you will rent a car call your auto insurance agent and inquire if you are covered while renting a car.

If you are covered then decline all coverage's at the rental agency. They make a lot of money on this insurance and it is a waste to purchase it. When in a foreign country you should buy auto insurance coverage if you rent a car. The rental agencies use tricks to get you to take the insurance so you have to be aware. They will say something like "do you want limited or full coverage on your car today"? You have to know to say I decline or I waive all coverage.

Life insurance

- The purpose of insurance in general is to cover a risk you cannot otherwise afford.
- Typically the first time you need life insurance is when you have your first child.
- Buying term insurance rather than universal life or whole life. Universal and whole life policies are cash value policies, and they charge a higher rate for the insurance.
- With term insurance if you change policies every two to five years, you are typically rewarded with a 30-50% reduction in your premium. This is because you must pass new health proving you are a lower risk.
- Large associations can have excellent deals, often not requiring you to change insurers every few years to get a better deal.
- As you get older, using a ten year level premium may be more convenient.

Income protection insurance

- Shortly after you borrow money or sign up for a credit card you are often offered an income protection insurance policy. These have fancy names like "Family Protection Plan" that will pay off your balance if you were to die or become disabled. Is this a smart purchase? No, these are typically very expensive life or disability insurance policies. If you want that coverage get it directly.

Disability insurance

- Disability insurance is something a professional might buy. Medical and dental professionals buy most of these policies because if they were injured they would have a greater difficulty continuing in their profession as compared to an accountant or attorney.
- The earlier in your career you purchase this policy the lower the premium. Typically you will have to increase the benefit amount several times over your career by either increasing your existing policy or adding a second policy.
- Professional associations often have favorable polices.
- Find and use a good insurance broker.

"The core of your personality is your self-esteem, "How much you like yourself." The more you like and respect yourself, the better you do at everything you attempt."
- Brian Tracy

Chapter 6 – Spending

How many pairs of shoes do you really need?

Controlling what you spend is a necessity. Managing your impulses takes discipline. We are bombarded with messages everyday that tell us to buy, spend and treat ourselves today. We are told we will be judged as a person by how we appear. We are conflicted by these messages because we know in our hearts that life is really about happiness and making a meaningful contribution to our family and society.

Your needs are basically the same no matter where you live. These are air, food, water, clothing, shelter, safety and movement. You create your "wants" from your friends and the culture in your community.

Wants are the things you would like to have. How much of these things does it take for efficiency and comfort? Your answer typically depends on where you live right now, not where you grew up. Of course we are all individuals with personalities and beliefs that are unique to us but not separate from our community.

If you live in a major metropolitan city in the U.S. like New York, Los Angeles, Miami, San Francisco, Chicago, Dallas, or San Diego you would typically have a higher set of expectations for the kind of car you drive, the amount and quality of things you own and the quality of home or apartment you live in or own.

If you lived in an environmentally conscious city like Portland, Seattle, or Denver you (the same person) would have a different view on what you need. If you took this a little further and moved to a small town with 3,000 people you would want much less. If you lived on a ranch an hour or more from a city you would want even less. If you lived in a rural Australia farm town you would want even less. How about if you lived in a rural town in China?

I have lived around the world and been amazed at the difference in myself in each of these environments. I am the same but my environment and what everyone else does influences what I want.

Our wants and spending patterns seem so fixed. Yet if we had to change we could. If we moved to a new environment we would change. The culture we live in has a strong influence on our beliefs.

What you should take from this is that you are always capable of changing how you spend money. When you feel like your spending cannot be changed it is because you have spent a long time in the same culture and situation. You are only unable to see the possibility of doing life in a different way. Necessity has a way of helping you change these rigid beliefs in a short time.

If you are reading this book you already enjoy more than 90% of all other people alive today at your age. You are fortunate enough to be in a position to ask the most important question of all – *"what am I here for"*. I answer this question with - I am here to further humankind with my special gifts. I also want to be happy doing that. Accumulating more shoes is not going to improve my contribution to humankind nor will it genuinely give me happiness today.

How much discount?

The general rule is it costs the original manufacturer of a product 10% to 20% of what something sells for retail. Not all goods have the same markup. Commodity items like computer hardware have smaller markups than branded or luxury items. Items that go straight from manufacturer to user or through only one middleman have fewer markups.

Do you think that the department stores are losing money when they sell jewellery at 70% off? Of course not! They are still making a small profit otherwise they would not do this every year.

Most items go through several middlemen. Some middlemen get a 25% markup, others 100%. The final retailer usually gets a markup called keystone. They buy something for $50 and sell it for $100. Fast moving items get less markup, slow moving items need a bigger markup.

How much does it cost to make and distribute a bottle of water today? A typical bottle of 16 ounces of water sells for $1.25 a bottle. The cost to the factory where it is made was around $0.06, most of which is the cost of the bottle and packaging, not the purified water itself.

The manufacturer sells each bottle for $0.10 to a distributor, 10,000 bottles at a time. He pays for shipping. The distributor usually sells the water delivered to the retailer for $0.20 to $0.60 each depending on the retailer's volume and negotiation ability. Wholesalers like Costco will buy it for $0.18 delivered from the factory to their distribution centers, and sell it for $0.24 each in cases of 24, from there you have to deliver it to your own store. Water is not usually sold on sale; however its price varies based on where you buy it.

A 14k gold ring with a ½ carat sapphire is manufactured for 1/20th its retail price. A large chain store that retails jewelry will buy this for 10% to 20% of its retail price. It will usually discount its jewelry 25% to 35% to anyone who asks. Of course if you do not ask you do not get the discount. Even jewelry that is on sale for 40% can be discounted further by bargaining. You may only get 10% more but the point is they may have more to give, but you have to ask. First, you have to know this is possible. Many high end luxury items can be discounted further at purchase.

Bargain on a snowboard?

First thing you should know is all ski, snowboard, and, for that matter, sporting goods are readily discounted 20%, even before Christmas.

Some items have fewer markups from manufacturer to retailer. Thus, they are discounted less to you, initially and at closeout. A $100 snowboard glove from Burton snowboards costs around $10 to make in China, and add another $2 for shipping, customs, local freight and stocking. Burton sells it for $60 to the retail store, who discounts it 20% to you, for a purchase price of $80. This retailer makes $20 per glove or 33%. If the store discounts the glove by 50% it loses $10 a glove or 17%. Burton makes $46 or 400% on their cost. Burton can get away with it because of branding.

Another snowboard manufacturer is looking to get established. They offer a similar high performance glove made in a similar factory in China with slightly different materials and styling. This glove costs $11 (because of lower volume) to make and another $2 for shipping etc. This glove retails for $80 and is sold to the store for $30. The store discounts it 20% so you buy it for $64. The store makes $34 off this glove or 113%. If the store discounts this glove by 50% it still makes $10 or 33%.

There are several methods to getting a deal on snowboard gear. I start with identifying what I want. Then I look for a deal on that item. For instance I wanted a Dynastar 4807 powder snowboard. Problem was it was selling retail for $680 to $780, a couple of hundred more than most boards. At the end of last season I found an eBay closeout and bought a few of them for $120 each ($20 under his lowest asking price, because I ordered a few for friends at the same time)!

I have a favorite snowboard shop that gives me 30% off all the time except the two weeks before Christmas. I get 40% off on all last years stuff. My favorite time for a discount is September, they really need cash and are closing out last years stuff.

Another technique is to get help buying from people who get a great discount in their job.

Then there are the blowouts of liquidated merchandise when a store closes. Knowing the insiders can help you get advance notice of these sales. I love buying a $400 jacket I need for $75 or $120 gloves for $25.

Loss leaders

An advertisement by our local snowboard retailer has a low quality glove on sale for $15 dollars. They paid $15 for this glove. They do this to get you in to buy other things that cost more, like a new snowboard.

Bait and switch

The local snowboard dealer offers this lower quality glove at only $15. They put the more expensive gloves up front and at eye level.

The sales people are trained to explain the difference between the sale gloves and the better gloves in a way that is likely to get you to want to buy the better gloves.

The art of getting a deal

Getting a fabulous deal starts with wanting to figure out how to get a deal on items that you need or really want.

Getting a deal in the U.S. is easy, sales are everywhere. It makes you wonder why anyone pays full retail. The selling system in the U.S. is flexible, well organized and operates in systematic patterns. When can you get the best deal on a winter coat? In early December, April or September? Just about anytime other than December through mid February.

What if you needed a new winter coat in early December how would you go about it? There are always ways. It starts with knowing what it is you want and then finding out where you can get it at a deal. Last year's model is always a good bet, many places will give you 40% off last year's stuff they still have in early December. You have to ask as they want you to buy this year's model at full price or only 20% off retail.

New vs. used

Some things are almost as good used as they are new, like furniture. Laptops are not a good idea used.

Garage sales have bargain basement prices. This can be a good place to shop for Christmas presents as well. Go to a little better neighborhood than you live in, and go early, even before they say they are open. Furniture deals can be a steal at a garage sale. Some people call on furniture or even go on Friday instead of Saturday. At first the sellers object when you come early, but it is a competitive game for the best stuff like furniture.

Consignment clothing stores can be a good deal for designer clothing.

Wholesale vs. retail

I love to buy wholesale. One of the best places to do that is at wholesale clubs like Costco. Sure you have to buy a larger amount. In college extra supplies can get used by others who do not always pay their fair share.

Quality at wholesale outlets varies as well. Some things are excellent quality and others are questionable.

Pirated software, DVD's and music

Go to China and you will find all the latest CDs, DVDs and software on sale for $1 or $2 instead of the $16 to $30 price you will pay in the U.S. How do they do that? Plain and simple these are illegal copies. Since China does not have a software industry, movie industry or music industry they do not yet police the copying of these items.

If everyone did this software development would stop, movies and music quality would drop dramatically. Without copyright protection books and any original art work would not have value. Without value it would not get shared, and no one could make a living at these businesses.

Illegally copying of music, DVDs and software can get you in trouble. If you are prosecuted this will end up on your permanent record and can interfere with your ability to get a good job or practice in certain professions.

Long Distance

If you have a land line telephone you need to signup for a long distance carrier and not just default to the service that comes with your phone. If you fail to signup for service the default service will cost you around $0.30 cents a minute. Today it is easy to get long distance for $0.07 cents a minute or even as low as $0.03 a minute without any monthly fee.

Cell Phone

For most of you this was your first real lesson in how the real world has financial rules and consequences. Cell phones and cell phone billing services are not perfect. You are far better off signing up for more minutes than you use, than going over and paying a per minute charge. If you did not have long distance and no roaming in your plan you are going to need it soon. Most students today can get by with a cell phone and no land line if they have high speed Internet.

High Speed Internet

I have been able to get by very nicely using a high speed Internet connection and a digital telephone service rather than the traditional land line. The cost savings over a land line can be substantial in some states.

I cannot imagine not having high speed Internet service today for web surfing. If you have roommates there are two ways to share, either using a wired Cat 5 router (back of a wireless router) or a wireless connection. If you do not password protect your wireless connection then neighbors can hook into your connection slowing your surfing down. As long as you have a firewall they cannot hack into your system even though they share your connection to the Internet.

Online Price Checks

First, compare prices at websites such as http://shopping.com, http://BizRate.com, http://PriceGrabber.com or http://MySimon.com.

Second, go to http://Google.com and type in the name of the product and the word rebate or coupon to see if any discount offer exists.

Online Reviews

Other consumers can offer better information than professional reviewers about products they have actually used. http://epinions.com has good information. Going to Google and typing in quotes "review of Sony digital camera" will lead to professional reviews, some by sellers. Another good site is http://consumerworld.org.

Chapter 7 - Your Identity & Money

Why should you worry?

According to a recent Federal Trade Commission (FTC) survey one in eight respondents were victims of identity theft in the last five years. In 2003 alone ten million Americans were victims of identity theft. These figures may be low as not all identity thefts are reported and counted.

The FTC found that the average loss of a person who had a new account opened by identity theft was $1,200. The average loss was $500 for all victims of identity theft.

Many victims are not sure how the theft actually happened and are unaware for some time that their identity has been stolen. According to the Identity Theft Resource Center (ITRC), 85 percent of fraud victims do not find out about the crimes committed against them until months later when they are typically applying for new credit. Others do not find out until they get a collection call.

A significant portion of the Internet fraud taking place today has its roots in the Russian Mafia according to WinPress News in August 2004.

It can take a lot of time to clear up an identity theft. The amount of time ranges from 1 hour to 250 hours of your time. This depends on how quickly you discover the problem. It is not unusual for it to take as long as a year to clear up your credit. The process can be most aggravating, especially if you are trying to get a loan or credit card as you try and clean up your credit.

Online auction fraud

By far the most common fraud found in the FTC database is online auction fraud. This is where you receive an official looking email saying you need to update your online account information for some official sounding reason. The crooks have a new reason every few weeks. One of the most popular targets has been eBay and PayPal. What they are really want is your PayPal user ID and Password. This gives them direct access to either your checking account or credit card.

The email looks exactly like an official email, including logo. The email return address will usually be an authentic address, but the email says "do not reply". Instead you are requested to follow the link provided to update your information so your service can continue.

This type of personal ID data gathering is called *"phishing"*. The very real looking email is called *"carding or brand spoofing"*. These can be modeled after any bank, credit card or other financial related entity like Quicken or PayPal. The email, logos and everything else including the reply address are all official looking. If you reply by clicking on the link and giving out your information, access to your bank account or credit card has been stolen and your identity information has been taken.

EBay and PayPal have been particularly hard hit by this. Here is the link to eBay's security center information website for examples of eBay spoofing. http://pages.ebay.com/securitycenter/index.html

If you want to see examples of the latest spoofs check out the Fraud Watch International website. It you get a questionable email, do not click on any link!. If you are curious if the email was a spoof you can look here in a couple of days. http://fraudwatchinternational.com This website is required reading.

Spoofing also happens to accounts where you have a saved credit card file and personal information. Examples would be http://Amazon.com, http://Fedex.com, http://UPS.com and just about any other major online retailer. Here the *phishing* seeks to get your User ID and Password through some phony account maintenance request. Once a crook has that it can access your stored personal information. Many of these companies have now protected your credit card number in their database and only show the last four digits when you access your account information.

You need to be very suspicious all the time about emails you receive. Do not EVER respond to account maintenance requests by clicking on the link in an email.

The best rule is to NOT click on any email links, even when these look to be from people you regularly do business with. Any of these emails are fair game to be spoofed. The best way to access your bank, PayPal, credit card or investment accounts is by links in your "Favorites" folder or by typing in their address in your web browser.

This may take a little more time but the first time you lose $500 and spend 6 months clearing up your credit report you will understand this requirement.

Mailbox theft

The next most common fraud is mailbox theft of personal ID information or checks. Un-cashed checks, particularly outgoing checks in your mail are stolen and *"washed"*. Here the signature is left on the check but the ink used to write the payee and sometimes the amount is washed off the check. The criminal then makes the check out to himself.

This actually happened to me a couple of years ago. Fortunately, the criminal was caught in the act of depositing several of these at once. I got a call from a bank teller asking me to verify one of my checks that was being presented for cashing. I confirmed this check was for a different payee and for a different amount. She was arrested at the bank. A few weeks later the police asked me to fill out a report. I was also asked to appear in court for the trial, but instead I filled out a written statement. She was convicted and sentenced to jail.

Fortunately for me this was stopped before any withdrawal took place from my account.

Here are some things you can do to protect yourself against this kind of fraud.
- ◆　Do not put outgoing mail in your mail box.
- ◆　Get a locked mail box.
- ◆　When you order checks by mail have them sent to a secure location, a locked mail box or to work.
- ◆　Download your bank and credit card information and pay attention to the charges.

♦ Retrieve your mail daily and as soon as possible after it is delivered.

Dumpster diving

The most common way criminals can get your identity is from a garbage can. Job applications, tax returns, loan applications, and year end tax reports all have your identity information (name, address and social security number). These discarded papers can be stolen from the trash cans of either an individual or a businesses.

You can protect yourself from this kind of identity theft by shredding all information you have with this sensitive information on it. Include applications for credit mailed to you in this list of what to shred.

EBay and PayPal transactions

Most eBay transactions are completed without a problem. But the rate of growth of eBay and PayPal fraud is rapid. You need to be aware of what thieves are doing today in this marketplace. EBay, email solicitation and the Internet are truly buyer beware environments.

EBay buyer story:

(Actual story of a disabled man)
I have been using eBay and PayPal for several years. I have been pretty good at avoiding problems. I always look for good feedback before bidding. I bid on a computer video card from a person (company) with very good feedback, and only one neutral feedback. I paid $113 using PayPal. In the next few days, the feedback started to show that the seller wasn't communicating with the buyers. Then eBay suspends him. The Seller is leaving messages to the effect that he went out of town on a family matter. He refuses to communicate any further.

PayPal puts my complaint on 10 day hold giving this guy 10 days to remedy this situation. He never communicates, and PayPal then tells me they cannot get my money back. EBay just gives you a canned response that says wait 30 days and do blah, blah, blah... then file for Buyer Protection (eBay owns PayPal) only difference is eBay will charge $30 for the 'Buyer Protection" but only after 30 days. I looked up more information on the person, company that disappeared with my money (eBay will not tell you anything about anyone when you get ripped off, you have to dig yourself). I never got my money back.

When checking feedback you must determine that the feedback is from selling not just buying activity.

EBay seller story:

This story was taken and simplified from an eBay warning website. This individual went to use his PayPal account on June 23 to pay for an eBay auction and discovered that my account had a negative balance of $1,504.75.

Here is his story told in the first person: On April 22 the thief sends me an email regarding a laptop I am selling on eBay. He asks if I would be willing to send the laptop to Russia. I state if he ends the auction with Buy-it-Now and pays the higher shipping rate I quote using USPS website quotes, I will. I get an email from PayPal that I have been paid $1,550.00 for this auction. The email shows the buyer is a verified buyer but no shipping address is provided. The buyer sends me an email telling me he paid the $1,550 and provides his shipping address.

I initiate a transfer from PayPal to my checking account, the transfer is confirmed. I send the package with a tracking number and email the tracking number to the buyer (thief).

May 28: the PayPal charge of $1,550 is reversed by the rightful PayPal account owner. It has been over a month since I received my cash from PayPal and I have received no communication from them. (The thief apparently stole the PayPal account user name and password to make this purchase using a spoof email).

June 23: while attempting to send money with PayPal for an unrelated eBay purchase I am notified my account has a negative balance and I must transfer the additional $1,504.75 to cover the negative balance, I abort the payment. To this point I still have not received an email, letter or telephone call from PayPal regarding this matter.

My series of telephone calls with PayPal results in being told I owe this money and must pay as I did not send the item I sold to a *confirmed PayPal address*. I file a fraud complaint with the Internet Fraud Complaint Center and USPS (both a good idea).

July 16: PayPal denies my claim and says they settled their investigation and sided with the buyer, as I was unable to provide signed proof of delivery, and they charged me an additional $10 charge for a back settlement fee.

July 24: PayPal sends a payment demand.

August 21: PayPal tells me I breached their user agreement by not paying and that attorney's fees and finance charges will continue until paid.

December 5: I get a call from a collection agency stating my PayPal account has been turned over to them. I explain my story again and tell them I refuse to pay. They say my account will be turned over to another attorney to collect.

December 9: I get a letter from the new attorney. I send a letter back saying I am not responsible for the insecurity of PayPal's website and will not pay.

March 15: I have not heard anything and apply for a loan. My credit report comes back without any mention of this item.

June 3: I close the loan and still no mention of this amount owing.

This individual says he gets one email a day from people in a similar situation who read his posting.

Western Union wire transfer fraud:

Beware if you buy something and the seller offers you a discount to make a wire transfer payment to Western Union. Many eBay frauds are based on this scam, especially overseas frauds. Do not wire transfer funds to any seller you do not know and have not done business with before. Once they get this money you have no protection.

EBay hacker of the year award
Story from http://empiresecurity.com, they report on thefts like found on eBay. Top selling items like Apple computer laptops are a prime target for eBay fraud.

Item listing:
The item is new, sealed in the original box and comes with 1 (one) year US warranty, and is shipped insured. We are a U.S. founded company with stores in Spain, Italy, Germany, France, Switzerland, Sweden, Norway, England and Ireland.

Our main store is in Malaga, Spain. Our policy for ecommerce does not allow up to ship Internet sales directly from our stores. We agreed with eBay (as well as with other auction sites like uBid and Yahoo that for our higher priced items (like laptops, camcorders, plasma TVs, etc)) we would warehouse at their regional warehouse. Using this method both buyers and sellers are insured by eBay's Square deal program. Your item will be shipped from eBay's warehouse in San Jose, CA. This is a pre-approved auction that means you are not allowed to bid or buy until your payment is completed.

Your payment must be sent to our sales manager "Sidney Webster". Our store address is: Plaza San Francisco 133, 29008 Malaga, Spain.

We prefer Western Union payment service. Western Union has many years in the money transfer business with locations worldwide. The transfer fees are charged to the sender and funds are available within minutes worldwide. The transaction is easy with no bank accounts or lengthy procedures, and Western Union has a proven track record and the ability to do transactions 7 days a week, 24 hours a day with a high level of security. EBay will send you a confirmation email as soon as you ask a question as "Question the Buyer" for backup legitimacy of our auction.

A potential buyer then hits the "Question the Buyer" button and asks a question. This actually goes to the "thief" not to eBay. The seller then sends back a response that looks like it came from eBay. The response goes something like this:

Dear eBay member,
We have been asked by "thief' to inform you about the legitimacy of his auction transactions. We advise you to close this specific transaction using the new Western Union and eBay secured program. We have the item you request in our warehouse ad and it will be shipped to your address from San Jose, California, when the seller has confirmed he has been paid by Western Union. You will not be allowed to bid or "Buy it Now" until payment is completed. *(This is why they got the fraud of the year award).* We adopted this method for both the buyer's and seller's protection. We insure the total price of the items sold by this seller and advise you to close this transaction.

Here is what you do next: The buyers and sellers should contact each other within three business days to complete this transaction. Buyers should send payment directly to the seller by Western Union wire transfer, if you need help click here: http:// cgi3.ebay.com/aw-cgi/eBayISAPI.dll?MemberSearchShow (a legitimate link). Once you complete the transaction please leave feedback at: http://cgi2.ebay.com/aw-cgi/eBayISAPI.dll (a legitimate link).

PayPal Lawsuit Settlement
(As reported by San Francisco Chronicle June 15, 2004)
EBay, the online marketplace, has agreed to pay $9.25 million to settle a class-action lawsuit that accused its PayPal payment service of mishandling customer complaints about fraud. All Pay-Pal users who held an account between Oct. 1, 1999, and Jan. 31, 2004, will be eligible for a payout.

The suit, filed in a federal court, said that PayPal routinely failed to respond to customer complaints about fraud or account errors. When PayPal did react, the suit said, it sometimes froze customer accounts for excessive periods of time. As part of the settlement, eBay agreed to provide customers more detailed disclosures when they register for a PayPal account, investigate account errors more quickly and provide users quarterly account statements by email. Some of the changes have been in place for some time.

Internet identity theft

If you get email spam offering to sell goods it may be a scam to get your credit card number, expiration date, security codes, and billing address. There is no way of knowing for sure if you are dealing with a legitimate business or not when responding to spam mail.

Secure server

All financial transactions must be done over a secure server. Never give out your credit card number without one. A secure server (Secure Sockets Layer – SSL connection) is indicated by two things. The closed lock icon at the bottom of your browser is the first, but it is not enough, make sure the web address is *https://*, the (s) standing for secure, not *http://*.

If you have to send someone your credit card information via a fax or email these are not secured and this information can be intercepted and stolen. If you have to send information at least split up the number and the expiration date into two emails or faxes..

419 Scams – The Nigerian Bank hustle

These are requests for help in completing a financial transaction and offering to give you a large commission for helping. This scam started decades ago as letters saying an estate needed settling or government funds needed to be settled in a bank outside of the country of origin, usually Nigeria, but now just about anywhere.

I personally get one a week in my junk email. I know what they look like and so I immediately discard them. The FBI processes around 500 complaints a day of people who have been bilked by these schemes.

They used to be for outrageous amounts of money, like $20,000,000. They you offered 10% or 20% to help clear these funds for the estate or the government official. What they are after is either upfront fees or a power of attorney to wire funds from your checking account. In either case the only money that changes hands is yours to theirs. It all sounds so simple for you to make some easy money.

Cashier's check scam

Scams are as varied as the grains of sand on a beach. The amount of money involved has dropped dramatically in the newer scams to make them seem more legitimate. Recently I advertised a sporting good item for sale on a small specialty website (http://extremebigair.com). The buyer was from Europe and at first offered to pay me $50 extra to accept a cashier's check from someone who owed him money in the U.S. as his way of paying for these goods. All I needed to do was help him out and mail him a check for the difference, about $2,000.

Lucky for me I refused. He then offered to pay me twice the asking price for my item to help him out. Again I refused. Finally, he told me his wife just had surgery and that is why he had not emailed me for a few days; he really needed my help with this cashiers check to pay her medical bills. Now I knew I had made the right decision earlier so again I refused and the emails stopped.

About 10 days later ExtremeBigAir.com sent out an email warning of this scam. Lucky for me I have made it a rule to only do business via the Internet the straight forward way. At the time I was most trusting of cashier's checks, now I know that they can be fake, just like any other check. You must wait at least 5 business days after depositing any check, even a cashier's check before you know the funds are good. Even PayPal payments can be refused within three days.

Bogus escrow accounts

Wire your money into a bogus escrow account and it is gone forever. Here a seller offers to protect you by putting your money into an escrow account until you receive the goods and sign-off that they are as advertised. You are told you must release the money from escrow.

There are legitimate escrow services out there. EBay has an escrow service with a very low fee that seems a good choice if you are doing a larger transaction overseas.

Western Union – secret answer scam

This works like an escrow account or so you are told. You send money to buy something and it is not released by Western Union until you give Western Union your *"Pass Phrase"*. There is no such arrangement like this with Western Union so as soon as your money gets there it is gone and the goods were never mailed to you in the first place.

Personal theft

Pick pockets:

Pick pockets are a serious and plentiful problem on the streets of Europe. It can also happen in the U.S. at crowded places like a concert. Even your front pocket is not safe unless your hand is in it at all times. These guys are professionals at bumping you and removing your wallet. Often they disguise themselves as beggars and work in teams. Other times they are dressed as business men. A money belt works well if kept under your pants or skirt. Fanny packs are open invitations, and they can unzip, remove and re-zip in a brief moment.

What car is stolen the most?

Is it a Ferrari, Lexus, BMW or Mercedes Benz? No the most stolen car is actually one of the most common ones. Honda Accords are the most stolen car in most cities in the U.S. today. Toyotas are also high on the list. These cars are stolen for parts.

Never leave your keys in your car! Never leave your car running while you are not in it. Did you know if you rent a car and it is stolen and you do not have the keys, you just bought it?

Personal belongings:

The items most often stolen in a home break in are items that can be sold at a pawn shop for cash to buy drugs. This includes con-sumer electronics, jewelry, computers and collectibles.

Laptops:
A laptop is easily stolen and easily sold for quick cash. Unfortunately, it could have your banking and personal identity information.

Purses:
Purses and day timers are prime targets at airports, discos, and restaurants.

Discarded computers:
Did you know that even if you reformat your hard drive recovery software can restore the data files? This is so easy that even your grandmother could use freeware to recover your erased data files.

You can download (freeware) or buy software that permanently deletes files. You can do this for all of your data files when you are discarding your hard drive. What most of these do is to write over your files up to a hundred times with random numbers. This finally makes your hard drive free from any kind of data recovery.

When you sell, gift or dispose of a hard drive you either must use this kind of software or remove and smash the hard drive to render it inoperable.

Just throwing the computer in the city garbage dump does not work. There it will be salvaged and the hard drive removed and sold. If you are unlucky it will be bought with thousands of others to be scanned for sensitive personal data by a new kind of thief.

Friends on drugs
When a friend, even your best friend gets addicted to hard drugs they are going to need money wherever they can find it. This means your wallet; credit cards and personal possessions can be stolen to get a fix. Just because they are a good friend does not make you immune, in fact it makes you vulnerable. It starts with lies and then it grows from there into petty theft and finally into larger thefts. It is easy to be in denial and even easier to become a victim and lose your friend forever.

Spyware

If you surf the web or if you receive spam email you get spyware inserted onto your computer, even when you have spyware protection software (different from anti-virus protection software).

Spyware is any software that employs a user's Internet connection in the background (the so called "backchannel" connection) without their knowledge or explicit permission.

Spyware comes in different flavors. The spyware agent can be "malware" that modifies system settings, and can perform undesirable tasks on your computer. "Hijacker" redirects your browser to websites. "Dialer" dials a service most likely a porn site, for which you are billed. "Trojan Horse" is attached to a program (many viruses use a Trojan Horse to get on your system) and can performs complex tasks as it installs software. "Collectware" collects information about you and your web surfing habits.

Today the most common issue with spyware is that it can slow your computer down to barely functional levels, at times. If your Internet connection is crawling fairly regularly and then working fine other times this could be your problem.

Most spyware is used by marketing firms to find out what websites you visit so they can target market to you. Cookies are the basis for Collectware. This is what the anti spyware programs find most regularly on my system. These are pretty harmless, except for what it does to your system's Internet speed from time to time.

There are many spyware removal utilities, some are freeware (you do not have to pay for them) and others cost around $20. I have used three spyware protection software "Norton Internet Security" http://Symantec.com "SpyBot" http://spybot.com and "Adware" http://Lavasoft.com to protect me from spyware attacks. Norton's is the least effective today. I liked SpyBot the best. Beware that some spyware detection software can disable needed functionality on your computer.

The worst form of spyware is used for identity theft. This software records keystrokes and reports those to someone without your knowing. All keystrokes are recorded including Internet surfing.

Viruses

Viruses come as an executable attached to an email, even email from your friends. Basically any executable attached to an email can be a virus. Do not click on anything attached to an email unless you trust it. If you click on an attachment you could be allowing a virus or application to install on your computer unless you are properly protected.

Virus attacks are a terrifying fact of life with spam mail. Computer repair shops today report as much as 80% of their work load comes from repairing computers infected with a virus(es).

Your best protection is to always have a program like Norton Internet Security (firewall and virus protection) installed and up to date on your computer. It is a required cost of using a computer today and protecting your privacy. It is NOT optional.

Email virus protection

A simple but effective trick that prevents your email list from being hijacked by a virus is to add a new name listing called "!000" to your address book. This will be your first listing. The software used by hackers to auto generate emails from your mailing list cannot get by this first name.

This name "!000" also blocks you from doing a name search by typing in the first letter of the alphabet you want the address book to jump to. Instead, you must first click on a name in the address book and then type the letter you want the address book to jump to. This is a small inconvenience to protect your address book from unauthorized email going out with viruses to all your friends, family and business relations. I learned this trick after a virus got my email list and replicated itself to everyone on my contact list. It has never happened again - more than seven years later.

Your identity - what information to protect
Social Security Number
Driver License Number

Credit Card Number, Expiration Date, Security Code and Password

Debit Card Number, Expiration Date, Security Code and Password

Mother's Maiden Name

Birthdate

Passwords

Limited Power of Attorney

Bank statements and investment statements

Your social security number is your personal identity. If that number gets into the wrong hands someone else can assume your identity for a time. With this they can do some serious harm to your credit rating. I experienced this first hand. My social security number was used by someone to rent an apartment. He skipped out and the landlord filed a notice with the credit agencies. This was relatively easy to clear up, as he used his name with my social security number.

My brother-in-law was not so lucky. Someone got his social security number and driver's license number from the California DMV. The "thief" signed up for a telephone service and never paid the bill. The bill came up to $1,600. My brother-in-law went to add a phone line and they would not let him without a $1,600 payment. That is how he first learned of this. It took him one year and 100 hours to get this off his credit report. Don't let this happen to you, guard your identity.

How to protect yourself

Only give your personal identification information out when absolutely required and to people you trust. Keep passwords secure. Never have passwords stored anywhere in your wallet.

It is a good idea to keep a password file to manage all your Internet and banking user names and passwords. If you use Word or Excel use both a password and an encryption program to secure this file. If you use a USB flash memory stick to carry files with personal information add encryption protection to this drive.

Shred paper with this information before throwing it away.

Resources for credit & theft information

Credit bureaus:

Equifax http://equifax.com   To order a report 800-685-1111
        To report fraud 800-525-6285
Experian http://experian.com
        To order a report or report a fraud 800-397-3742
TransUnion http://transunion.com
        To order a report 800-888-4213
        To report a fraud 800-680-7289

General ID theft:

Federal Trade Commission http://consumer.gov/idtheft
Identity Theft Prevention and Survival Site http://identitytheft.org
Identity Theft Resource Center http://intheftcenter.org
Identity Fraud complaint Center http://ifccfbi.org
National Association of Consumer Advocates http://naca.net/
resource.htm
Privacy Right Clearinghouse http://privacyright.org
619-298-3396
Social Security Administration http://ssa.gov
800-772-1213
U.S. Department of Justice Identity Theft and Fraud Information
http://usdoj.gov/criminal/fraud/idtheft.html
U.S. Department of State Passport Services http://travel.state.gov/
passport_services
U.S. Postal Inspection Service http://usps.com/websites/depart/
inspect

Check fraud:

CheckRite 800-766-2748
ChexSystems 800-428-9623 or 800-328-5121
Cross Check 707-586-0551
Equifax 800-437-5120
National Processing Co. 800-526-5380
Scan 800-262-7771
TeleCheck 800-366-2425 or 800-710-9898
Your Bank

"One's philosophy is not best expressed in words; it is expressed in the choices one makes. In the long run, we shape our lives and we shape ourselves. The process never ends until we die. And, the choices we make are ultimately our own responsibility."

- Eleanor Roosevelt

Chapter 8 – Credit Rating

Credit score:

There are three main credit rating companies in the U.S. All lenders will look at your credit rating when considering you for a loan or for credit. Your credit scores determine your ability to borrow and at what rate.

If you sign up for a cell phone service, rent an apartment, get electrical service, buy a used car, obtain a credit card, apply for a job they may check your credit.

If you do not have a credit rating then they will require a deposit, require a co-signor, limit your credit, deny you credit, or refuse to employ you.

Your credit rating is based on your loan and credit repayment history as well as any utility bills that were sent in for collection.

You can establish a credit rating by taking out debt and making payments. Once you have a credit card and use it a few times you will have a credit report rating. Even if all you charged was $100 a month for a few months that would establish your credit rating. It is how you deal with the repayment of your debts that determines your credit rating, not the amount.

Any application for credit triggers a reported inquiry on your credit score. This helps other financial institutions see who else you might be applying to for a loan or credit card. If you have too many inquiries or too many new credit cards your score is lowered until these new credit cards are seasoned, usually six months.

The credit reporting agencies reflect adverse items for up to seven years.

Your credit score affects your ability to borrow, and most importantly it can help or hinder you in achieving your dreams. Seven years is a long time to wait for a mistake to be removed from your credit.

Many credit card sales people will tell you that you need a credit card to establish your credit. What they fail to tell you is if you are late or get behind in payments to your credit card this will damage your credit rating.

The best way to establish credit with a credit card is to pay your account in full each month. Carrying a balance does not improve your score and it could lower it.

Even if you get a new credit card offer that says "You are Pre-Approved" this does not obligate them to issue you the card. In the fine print they have an out based on your credit history.

Credit reporting agencies

- Equifax. http://equifax.com (800) 685-1111 P.O. Box 740241 Atlanta, GA 30374
- Experian. http://experian.com (888) 397-3742 P.O. Box 2002 Allen, TX 75013
- Trans Union. http://transunion.com (800) 916-8800 P.O. Box 34012 Fullerton, CA 92834

If you are denied credit you can get a copy of your credit report for free from any of the agencies listed above.

You can purchase your credit report at any time. You can also purchase an annual credit monitoring service that will notify you of any new negative items to hit your credit report. This is an expensive service, it costs around $10 a month today.

Credit reporting is social security number based. Cleaning up your credit report takes a lot of work, but it is worth it. If someone else's negative transaction is mis-reported on your credit you will have to dispute this transaction with one of the three credit reporting agencies that show the mis-reported transaction.

If you believe a lender has incorrectly reported a late payment you usually initiate this kind of a credit reporting error with the lender. Be sure to ask them to correct your credit report when they straighten out the problem.

If you are facing a particularly difficult situation you should seek the help of someone experienced in clearing up credit reports. Sometimes bankers can be of help. Other times you may need to hire someone experienced to review your situation and help you clear up the problem. Some of the problems can be fixed easily and others can take a year or more.

"Courage is what it takes to stand up and speak; courage is also what it takes to sit down and listen."

- Winston Churchill.

Chapter 9 - Passwords

One should have a strategy for setting up or establishing passwords. I recommend you use two or three categories of passwords (high, medium, low or high and low). Within each category have a different approach. When you change a password do so for all the accounts within that category.

You do not want to share your PIN number used for banking purposes with any person or nonfinancial website. Access to your checking account and credit cards must be protected.

There are situations where you may need to give out some of your passwords. Make sure those passwords are low security passwords. Do not give out high or medium security passwords to anyone.

A roommate or friend may need to use your laptop or get a file for your laptop. If your laptop requires a password to get to your files, this should be a low security password. It should in no way relate to your medium or high security passwords.

Password categories:
High security
Things you need to keep totally private and secure must be protected by a password that you never give out. Banks do not ask you for your ATM password, PayPal never asks you to verify your password. Use at least 8 digits, alpha and numeric whenever possible.
- ATM card / Debit Card password
- Credit card password
- Online banking password
- PayPal password
- Other banking password
- Your encrypted password file

Medium security
Things you need private and secure but the login could be entered

in a non-secure manner online.

- ◆ Websites where you have your credit card on file, like http:// Amazon.com, http://UPS.com.
- ◆ Personal Excel or Word files you wish to password protect.

Low security

These are passwords you use for access to information services, or to vendors, or in places you know you will possibly end up sharing your password with others.

- ◆ To access Internet services, other than ones with access to your banking, financial assets. Do NOT store your credit card information on their files.
- ◆ Low security computer files where you may give out the password to others.
- ◆ Computer login password at home or at the office to logon to the network.
- ◆ School registration / grades.
- ◆ Initial passwords you give out orally, that you will change later to a more secure password.

Passwords storage

There are software programs that store usernames and passwords. I prefer using an Excel spreadsheet and put a password protection and a 128 bit encryption on the file. It is important to add any new website username and password to this file each time you setup a new access. With practice I have become pretty good at this now. I use two worksheets one for my banking and high security passwords and one for all others.

"Never measure the height of a mountain until you have reached the top. Then you will see how low it was."

- Dag Hammarskjold

Chapter 10 – Financial Aid

Financial aid basics:
With good credit, you can usually afford to go to your school of choice.

Checklist of things to do:
- Talk with the financial aid office at your school.
- Speak with your parents. You need to know how much they will contribute. Will they co-sign for loans? Will they borrow money for you?
- You must understand the financial aid process. The more you know about the financial aid system, the better your chances of success.
- Start early and know the deadlines. This process has very strict deadlines and timelines.
- Don't automatically rule out high-cost schools.
- Obtain a financial aid package from the schools you are applying to.
- Use the Internet resources like these:
  http://estudentloan.com
  http://student-loans.com
  http://studentloan.com
  http://mapping-your-future.org
  http://tgslc.org (Integrated Common Manual)
  http://canlearn.ca (Canadian Loan Information)
  http://studentloanconsolidator.com
  http://loanconsolidation.ed.gov
  http://slcp.com

Financial aid calendar
Senior year of high school
September - December
Apply for admission to your top school choices. Attend a financial aid workshop if one is available at your school. Apply for scholarships and grants.

January - March

File the Application for Federal Student Aid (FAFSA) and other forms required by your school(s). This can be filed over the Internet at http://www.fafsa.ed.gov.

January is a good time to contact the financial aid administrator at the schools you have applied to for information on aid application procedures. Schedule an appointment with your school's financial aid officer. Many colleges require forms to be submitted by early January or February.

If you are applying for an early decision or early action, colleges will want forms filed earlier then normal.

February 15th appears to be a priority deadline for applying for aid for many colleges and state aid programs. Most private scholarship applications are due in February. Missing priority deadlines may cause you to lose out on receiving aid.

February is when Student Aid Reports (SAR for FAFSA) will start coming in.

March is the month when students normally start narrowing their choice of a college. Students typically also update their SAR information in March.

April

In April you need to review the financial aid packages you have been offered by various schools. 35% of all school financial aid applications are verified as required by the Federal Government. If you are chosen to verify your information, do so in a timely manner.

May - June

May and June are the months when you must choose what school you will attend in the fall. You will also receive your school's financial aid package.

You will need to return your financial aid package to your school of choice. All Federal loans must be certified by the college's financial aid office to prove you are accepted for enrollment at that school for the next year.

If needed this is the time to find alternative or private sources to make up any funding shortfall.

August - September
Early August is when you will need to follow-up with the school's business office to make sure that your financial aid award has been credited to your account.

September (or late August) is when school starts. Any changes in your course total can impact your aid program.

Types of financial aid
Scholarships:
A Scholarship does not have to be repaid. A scholarship is generally awarded to a student from a private funding source based on financial need or for performance in academics, athletics and music. Ask your guidance counselor to help you get started, or check out the many Internet resources that help students find scholarships.

Grants:
Grants also do not have to be repaid. Grants are based on financial need. The largest grant program from the federal government is the Pell Grant (for undergraduates only). Pell Grants are reserved for the neediest students. The maximum Pell Grant is $3,000 for the school year. Supplemental Education Opportunity Grants are also available. These funds are disbursed at the campus level, and are also reserved for needy students. The State Student Incentive Grant program is a federal program that matches state grants to students. Again, it is reserved for needy students. Generally speaking, it is difficult to receive grants unless your family is financially challenged. Grants are competitive, so start applying a year in advance to improve your chances.

Student loans:
A student loan must be repaid. The bulk of financial aid is given out as a loan. "Federal" or "Government" student loans are admin-

istered and disbursed through two different programs.

The first one is the Federal Family Education Loan Program, or FFELP. This is administered through a network of commercial lenders. Your award letter will contain a list of approved lenders.

The second program, if applicable at your school, is the Ford Direct Lending Program (FDLP). Here the Federal Government is the lender.

Both programs are government (Federal) backed. Federal loans can either be subsidized or non-subsidized. In a subsidized loan, the government pays your interest expense while you are in school. With an non-subsidized loan, you pay the interest yourself. Subsidized loans are awarded based on financial need. Even if your parents are in a strong financial condition you can still be eligible for non-subsidized student loans.

Stafford loans:
The interest rate for Stafford loans is capped at (cannot exceed) 8.25 percent. Repayment of Stafford loans begins six months after you complete school.

Subsidized vs. non-subsidized loans:
Subsidized loans are given based on demonstrated financial need. When subsidized, the government pays the interest while the student is in school. If the student is classified as not being in financial need, then the interest will be charged from the time the loan is disbursed until it is paid in full.

PLUS loans:
PLUS loans are given to parents. There is no limit to PLUS borrowing, but repayment begins immediately after the loan is taken out. Parents can still ask the student to be responsible for paying these loans either during or after school, but the parent remains liable for this loan until it is paid in full.

The interest rate for a PLUS loan is calculated annually by adding 3.1 percent to the rate of the 52-week (1 year) U.S. Treasury Note.

The rate is capped at 9.0 percent for the life of the loan. A one time loan origination fee of 3.0 percent is charged by the Federal Government.

Perkins loans:
Perkins loans are similar to Stafford loans. Perkins loans are administered through your school directly from a fixed allocation by the government. Schools can allocate these funds as they see fit. Perkins loans are need based. Usually they carry a lower interest rate than Stafford loans.

Work-study:
The federal work-study program allows students to earn money by working at their school.

To receive financial aid you must be enrolled at least half time, and some schools require you are enrolled full time. Federal aid programs are usually restricted to US citizens, and permanent residents. If you are a male US citizen, and are 18 years of age or older, you must be registered with Selective Service to receive federal aid.

Dependent / independent students:
All schools use the same formula to determine how much Federal financial aid to award to students. The cost of education minus the Federal expected family contribution. The expected family contribution is: the student and parent incomes and assets (excluding the value of the parent's home). For independent students, only the student's (and spouse's) income and assets are considered. To qualify as an independent student, you must meet at least one of the following criteria:
- Be at least 24 years old
- Be an orphan
- Have a dependent other than a spouse
- Be a graduate or professional student
- Be a veteran of the Armed Forces
- Be married
- Be a ward of the court

Financial need:

- ♦ Cost of Attendance (COA) for your school.
- ♦ Expected Family Contribution (EFC), the amount of money your family is expected to contribute to your education.

Your financial need is the difference between your COA and EFC.

Your school's COA will include tuitio, fees, books and supplies, room and board, travel and personal expenses.

Schools have limited funds available for financial aid, and because of this they usually allocate funds based on need.

The EFC calculation for the parents includes both natural parents regardless of divorce. If the divorced parent remarries the new spouse's information must be included.

The EFC calculation of the student is usually 35 percent of the student's assets and 50 percent of the student's preceding year earnings. (The federal calculation is 35 percent of the student's assets and 50 percent of the net earnings above $2,200.)

The EFC calculation of the parent is based on the number of parents with earned income, their income, assets and a few other factors. Income is determined from the adjusted gross income from their tax return with adjustments for nontaxable income.

Student assets and income count much more than their parents. Thus, it is a good idea to save money for college in the parent's name rather than in the student's name. If you have a savings account setup by your parents or grandparents for college it is best to use that up when you first start school if you plan on applying for financial aid at some time for college.

As the number of family members in school goes up the EFC will go down.

Annual limits for Stafford loans:

	Dependent Students	Independent Students
1st Yr	$2,625	$ 6,625
2nd Yr	$3,500	$ 7,500
3rd Yr +	$5,500	$10,500
Graduate	$8,500	$18,500

Private or alternative loans

Private or Alternative loans can be used to make up any shortfalls in covering your educational costs. Do not just rely on the stated interest rate as upfront fees affect the actual cost. All lenders are required to reflect these fees in an overall interest rate calculation called the AFR rate. The AFR rate is the best way to compare the real interest rate for various loans.

All private or alternative lenders will do both a credit check and an income-to-debt ratio calculation. Your eligibility to receive these loans is based on this. A history of late payments can eliminate your ability to borrow money to go to college.

Caution on student loans

With the rapidly escalating cost of a college education it has become a business decision as well as a personal growth decision to go to college when you must take out loans. Not all professions pay well once you graduate. Consider carefully how long your chosen profession will take you to pay off your debt. A good rule of thumb is you should reasonably expect to have all your student loans paid off in 7 years or less. Remember these loans must be paid back with after tax dollars. If you are aiming for a career in a less lucrative field, like education, then you should attend a community college for your first two years and then plan on an instate State University for your second two years and your masters.

Consolidating loans

The rules just changed for loan consolidation after graduation. Due to the record low interest rates in effect for the last few years many students were able to consolidate their loans at graduation at record low rates and lock in this rate for the duration of their loans. After June 2006 this will no longer be allowed and only Variable Rates will be permitted in a consolidation loan.

The first thing you need to know is that you will have to pay these loans back. The federal government does not take kindly to non performing student loans. Lenders and the federal government have continued to increase the ways they have to get their money from dead beat borrowers.

It is a good idea to seek guidance from the school financial aid office about your specific facts and get help understanding your choices. If you are unclear about which option to go with, discuss your facts and options with your parents for their input. Ultimately this debt is your responsibility so make the decision that will best suit your long term situation.

Loan consolidation lets you combine all your student loans into one loan and convert variable rates into a fixed rate (ends June 2006). 2003 and 2004 have proven to be one of the best times to consolidate student loans into a single fixed rate loan. Consolidating your student loans has several advantages:
♦ Convert loans to a Fixed interest rate (ends June 2006)
♦ One check to write
♦ One lender to deal with
♦ Standard, Graduated or Income Sensitive Repayment Plans

The Federal Consolidation Program allows the following loans to be included in a loan consolidation.
♦ Subsidized Federal Stafford Loans
♦ Non-subsidized Federal Stafford Loans
♦ All Federal Direct Student Loans (Direct Loans)
♦ Federal Parent Loans for Undergraduate Students (PLUS)
♦ Federal Perkins Loans
♦ Health Profession Student Loans
♦ Health Education Assistance Loans (HEAL)
♦ Nursing Student Loans
♦ Federal Supplemental Loans for Students (SLS)
♦ Auxiliary Loans to Assist Students (ALAS)
♦ National Direct Student Loans (NDSL)

- Federally Insured Student Loans (FISL)
- Federal Consolidation Loans

Most Federal student loans have a variable rate of interest. Those rates are adjusted each year. A Federal consolidation loan can have a fixed rate of interest. The fixed rate is determined at the time of consolidation and is based on a weighted average of the interest rates you are paying on your current student loans.

It is very difficult to determine if or when interest rates will increase or decrease. In general as an economy improves interest rates rise. During economic slowdowns interest rates fall. It is impossible to time interest rate tops or bottoms despite what anyone says or you may believe. Not even the best interest rate forecasters can do this. Selecting a fixed or variable rate is an important decision and it should be made with the help of a family friend who is a seasoned and experienced banker or investment manager if at all possible, but remember even they cannot time the top or bottom of interest rates.

To guarantee success, act as if it were impossible to fail.

- Dorothea Brande

Chapter 11 - Renting

How much rent can you afford?

When selecting a place to rent your safety comes first. If a prospective rental does not provide adequate safety then no price is acceptable.

Spend a few hours going though the rental ads and a couple of days of visiting places and you will start to get an idea about what is available in each price range. If you write down each listing that catches your interest this also can help you figure out the price ranges faster.

Housing close to school usually costs more than a three bedroom house a couple of miles away shared with other students. The close in student apartment has a lot of advantages that make it a better starting place.

Roommates reduce the cost of rent, but come at a price. One roommate always keeps things cleaner than the other. One always pays their bills less reliably than the other. One always makes more noise than the other. One always brings more friends around than the other. One always uses more utilities than the other. One helps themselves to the other's food more than the other. Some of this is just life; some of it is an avoidable hassle.

On campus / off campus

Many people opt for on campus housing in their first year. It costs a little more, but it is far more convenient, and food is greatly simplified. It is a preferred transition for many students who are on their own for the first time.

Another favorable thing about on campus housing is you are surrounded by lots of other people in your same situation in life. This helps foster the development of friends and a new social life much faster.

Roommates

A rite of passage. Hopefully you will not have enrolled in the roommate from hell course. There are quite a number to experience if that is what you are into.

Cost savings, and personal growth together are the ideal goal of roommates. The learning you get here can help you with setting boundaries and rules for mutually beneficial coexistence. The lessons learned can help you in marriage, the work place and later in raising your children.

Roommates require that you set boundaries, and establish and enforce agreements. Roommates require communication and cooperation. The most important rule is to communicate about issues when they present themselves. Do this and problems will stay a lot smaller than if you fail to deal with things early.

Paying rent

Landlords and rental agencies are for the most part used to dealing with students. They can at times be abusive to students and take advantage of new students.

You can count on having to pay your rent on time every month. This is not a bill you can be late with. If you are getting your money from your parents to pay rent then have the money put into your account before the 1st as most rent is due on the first and you will hear from the landlord on the 2nd or shortly thereafter if it is not in on the 1st. The landlord likely has a mortgage payment that is due shortly after the 1st.

Rent is paid in advance. When you pay rent on the first it is for the month you just started. Most rental agreements require a 30 day notice for moving out or the end of the lease. When you move out you may get a refund of any unused days on your security deposit. This refund can take up to 30 days after you move out. Most landlords will get you a check within a week of your moving out, but some take the full 30 days or even more.

Have each roommate on the lease or rental agreement. It is an unacceptable risk for one person to rent the place in their name only. Violate this rule and you will find out the hard way why this is a necessary rule. The problem comes up when someone needs to leave or if someone cannot pay their rent. If they are not on the lease or rental agreement then they can make moving out your problem. Do this right in the beginning and things will go a lot smoother down the road.

Deposits
Deposits are required for rent and all utilities until you have established a good payment history. A typical deposit can be from 40 to 200 dollars. Your apartment landlord will require a rental security deposit of at least one month's rent in advance.

In order to get a full refund on your security deposit your rental needs to be in the same condition that you took possession of less any ordinary and expected wear and tear. It needs to be properly cleaned when you leave. If the carpet has stains it may need to be shampooed. Deposits are an area where the landlord can and sometimes will play games on new students. You can usually tell from your prior interactions with the landlord what this experience will be like. When a landlord was difficult to deal with along the way they will be even more difficult to deal with when you leave. If you suspect this is the case, do a little more than necessary and take pictures.

Always give your rental termination notice in writing. In general you should put all business dealings in writing. Anything to do with real estate must be in writing to be legally enforceable.

Utilities
Financially irresponsible roommates demonstrate their true nature when the time comes to pay the utility bills. This is an area where strict rules and consequences are required. Early warnings of bigger problems to come usually show up here first. Have each of the roommates sign up for one of the utilities.

How to get a good deal
There is a definite seasonality to the college housing market. At

the end of every school year a lot of housing is vacated. You will find the best places and the best rental rates in June and July. Wait until August to save a few bucks and your choices are greatly diminished and the costs are higher. In fact, the deal you find in June or July often pays for the extra month or two of rent and there is no substitute for a better situation.

"There is one quality which one must possess to win, and that is definiteness of purpose, the knowledge of what one wants and a burning desire to possess it."

- Ronald Reagan

Chapter 12 - Savings

Saving money every month from your paycheck is the most important money fundamental you must learn. I promised you at the beginning of this book that I would teach you how to be successful with money. This chapter will teach you how to do that.

Making a million dollars a year or more will not make up for not knowing this fundamental about money. If you want to be successful with money you need to practice the fundamental of saving a portion of what you earn.

In working with thousands of people around money and finances for many years as a financial advisor I have seen that invariably people who are successful with money are good savers and began saving and investing as soon as they started working.

If you want to make a real difference in your life around money and not live a life full of bad money habits and practices then learn how to save. As with most things in life this lesson is easiest to learn when you are young. I know some of you may find it hard to believe that it is possible to save money while you are working in college.

All lessons are easier to learn when you are young and open minded. Making more income does not make saving any easier. Not learning how to save when you first start working makes learning to save later in life harder. There is always a reason to put off starting to save, and the truth is it never gets easier once you develop the habit of procrastination around saving money.

Excuses I have heard include:
 ♦ I will start savings when I get out of college.
 ♦ I will start savings after I get a new car.
 ♦ I will start savings after I get a raise.
 ♦ I will start savings after we get married.
 ♦ I will start saving after we get new furniture.
 ♦ I will start savings after we setup the new bedroom for our first kid.

◆   I will start saving after we get a better apartment, house, boat, vacation home, the kids get out of private school, college and so the promise goes.

Learning how to save, and doing it month after month will teach you more about being successful with money than getting a CFP (Certified Financial Planner) license, becoming a stock broker, reading 50 books about money or listening to 500 hours of financial instruction on audio CDs.

All it takes to save is putting aside 10% of what you make out of every paycheck. If you always do this from the first time you start working I promise you that you will be a master of money and you will have mastery over money for your entire life. A short time after you learn to save I promise that you will be making enough money. Learn to save and money will not ruin your relationships.

I believe that the discipline necessary to live off 10% less than one makes creates on its own a healthy relationship with money. It controls and mitigates many of the money diseases that people fall into. It creates a balance between consumption and saving something for tomorrow. When you have this balance it mitigates the drive to have more and more things regardless of how much you make. Without this balance, the tendency to consume and acquire more things leads to a life of financial inadequacy regardless of your income.

If you only follow one thing I present in this book, this is the one to do. Save 10% of what you make from every paycheck for the rest of your life. Start this now and never stop, I promise it will empower you around money for as long as you live. It works like magic. The longer you do it the more it does for you. As a successful financial planner working with thousands of clients for many years I know this for a fact.

Savings and Investing
Savings – Pay Yourself First
The best way to save is to "Pay Yourself First". This is when you treat savings as a required activity – like paying your electric bill. "Pay Yourself First" is about learning to make your monthly saving

account additions mandatory, not discretionary.

Investing
This is what you do with the funds added to your savings accounts. It includes buying financial assets like stocks and bonds, real estate, a business, paying off debt in an accelerated manner, or parking the funds in a money market account.

Investing is when you buy things that will provide a future income stream or future appreciation that will some day be converted to an income stream.

Buying a house, for example, is not an investment *per se*. It will not provide you with a future income stream, unless you are planning to trade down at retirement, in which case the trade down portion is an investment.

Active or passive investor?
Passive investors are more focused on watching their account balance grow every month. They get genuinely excited by seeing the growth in their investment account regularly. They dislike seeing their account decline. They prefer more safety in their investments, but want good growth as well. They are often open to help from others, but still make their own decisions in the end.

The passive investor likes the traditional investment strategies of money market accounts, bonds, and stocks. High risk taking is not usually their approach.

Active investors are more into building things and taking more risk. They prefer spending to saving. They see a home as some-thing to fix up and buy for its investment potential. They are always looking for opportunities for growth. Saving money is just a means to an end. As soon as they have an investible balance they begin looking for ways to invest.

Active investors are risk takers. Sometimes they take too much risk or expect too much too soon. The key for an active investor is to do your research before you invest. Turning spending behavior into investment action requires a focus on buying things that will produce income. Real estate and business ownership are good choices for your savings, rather than just stock and bonds if you are an active investor type.

It takes savings to support either form of investor. Both types of investors can be financially secure, and it is helpful to know what kind of an investor you really are.

Saving example - IRA

This is an example of geometric progression. I created this to explain the power of starting your savings early. Both options earn 10 percent a year. In Option 1 you fund $3,000 a year into an IRA for only the first 8 years, then you stop making contributions but let it grow until year 40. In Option 2 you make no IRA contributions during the first 8 years. Starting in year 9 and continuing through year 40 you make 32 contributions of $3,000 each. Which strategy do you think produces a better result in the end, saving $24,000 or saving $96,000?

The Benefits of Starting to Save Early
(10.0% Compound Interest Rate)

Year	Contribution	Option 1 Balance	Contribution	Option 2 Balance
1	$ 3,000	$ 3,300		
2	3,000	6,930		
3	3,000	10,923		
4	3,000	15,315		
5	3,000	20,147		
6	3,000	25,462		
7	3,000	31,308		
8	3,000	37,738		
9		41,512	$3,000	$ 3,300
10		45,664	3,000	6,930
11		50,230	3,000	10,923
12		55,253	3,000	15,315
13		60,778	3,000	20,147
14		66,856	3,000	25,462
15		73,542	3,000	31,308
16		80,896	3,000	37,738
17		88,985	3,000	44,812
18		97,884	3,000	52,594
19		107,672	3,000	61,153
20		118,439	3,000	70,568
21		130,283	3,000	80,925
22		143,312	3,000	92,317
23		157,643	3,000	104,849
24		173,407	3,000	118,634
25		190,748	3,000	133,798
26		209,823	3,000	150,477
27		230,805	3,000	168,825
28		253,885	3,000	189,007
29		279,274	3,000	211,208
30		307,201	3,000	235,629
31		337,921	3,000	262,492
32		371,713	3,000	292,041
33		408,885	3,000	324,545
34		449,773	3,000	360,300
35		494,751	3,000	399,630
36		544,226	3,000	442,893
37		598,648	3,000	490,482
38		658,513	3,000	542,830
39		724,364	3,000	600,413
40		796,801	3,000	663,755
Total	**$ 24,000**	**$796,801**	**$96,000**	**$663,755**

The results from compounding $24,000 saved in the first 8 years over a 40-year period is superior to saving $96,000 over a 32-year period ($3,000 per year beginning in year 9 and continuing to year 40).

This chart demonstrates that with a constant rate of savings one-half of the money you will have 40 years from now will come from your first 8 years of savings! This is the proof that starting to save as soon as you begin working is the most reliable way to become financially independent.

What to save?
♦ 5 percent is a minimal savings level, start here and increase to 10 percent.
♦ 10 percent is an average saver – build yourself up to this saving level as soon as possible.
♦ 15 percent is a strong saver
♦ 20 percent or more is a power saver

How to save?
♦ Savings is a requirement. Treat it like a required utility or loan payment.
♦ Pay Yourself First. Automate your monthly savings once you have a full time job. Mutual funds like Vanguard will do an automatic saving withdrawal from your checking account for the same amount on the same day each month. You can fund a 401(k) retirement savings plan at work this way as well, usually after working full time for one year at a new job.

Where to save?
♦ Tax deductible saving accounts are best. This is true for two reasons. First, it is easier to save 10 percent of what you make when you get a tax deduction for your savings. Second, your investments grow free of income taxes until they are withdrawn.
♦ 401(k) plans at work are the best place because most corporations typically do a match of 50 cents for each dollar you save.

- IRAs, they are limited currently to 3,000 dollars a year or your earned income, whichever is less.
- For young savers Roth IRAs are usually preferable. They are nondeductible going in, and nontaxable coming out. While you have a low tax rate this is the best way to go.
- Regular IRA's are deductible when you fund them and taxable when you take your money out. When your federal marginal tax rate is 28% or more this type of IRA becomes preferable.

Personal savings

- When you start working full time I recommend each person build up a personal reserve equal to three months outflows. This type of account should be a money market savings account.
- Cars, vacations and other irregular purchases need to be saved for and paid for out of the personal reserve account.
- Home purchase fund - you will need 5% to 10% of the purchase price saved to purchase your first home. Banks will generally approve a purchase where the monthly loan payment on the home is no more than 28% of your combined annual income. This is called the front-end ratio. Banks have a second loan ratio called the back end ratio and here all of your monthly loan payments cannot exceed 36% of your combined monthly income. If you can make a 10.1% down payment banks will waive the high cost mortgage insurance requirement.

Savings programs

Since developing the saving habit is the most important skill you need with money, I have developed a program to get your parents support to succeed at developing this skill. This is a win-win game. You win and your parents win.

College IRA savings program:

- The parent matches all contribution to the IRA by the working student while they are in high school and college.
- Match amount: 1:1, 2:1, 3:1 or 4:1. For each dollar the student saves the parent matches it dollar for dollar, two for one, three for one or four for one. You have to negotiate the

match amount with your parents.

- IRA contributions are limited to the maximum of $3,000 a year or the total of your gross wages, whichever is less. If you made $2,000 in gross income and your parents agreed to a 3:1 match you would need to fund $500 to your IRA and with a match of three times that amount, which comes to $1,500. You could fund the maximum for that year of $2,000 (limited by your gross earned income).
- The commitment should be in writing. I have a PDF form ttp://healthywealth.com/articles/savings-game.pdf or Word document http://healthywealth.com/articles/savings-game.doc for this purpose on my website you can download and use for your personal use. All commercial use or reprinting of these forms requires written permission from me in advance.

High school / college car:

If your parents want you to pay for all or a portion of your car you need to setup a savings plan to get that car. Here your parents' match is done at the time of purchase rather than adding to your account as you go.

Early career savings game:

Since savings is the most important financial fundamental to learn I recommend supporting young adults in developing savings skills in their first two years after college as well.

IRA savings are the best for this purpose.

- For the first full calendar year after college your parents might agree to a 1:1 or 2:1 match to every dollar you put into their IRA account. At a 1:1 match you put in $1,500 and your parents match this with $1,500. For a 2:1 match you put in $1,000 and your parents match this with $2,000. You cannot afford not to save when you get this kind of help, it is just too good to pass up.
- For the second year, the matching amount should drop or stay at 1:1.

Chapter 13 – Investing

In college or just starting out in the work force you usually do not have much in the way of savings to invest. In fact you may have more debt than savings. But if you have followed my advice in the last chapter you should have an IRA and need to invest those funds.

Investing is for the long term. Long term is 15 or more years. When you invest you should ask yourself "is this a superior way to invest for returns over the next 15 years"?

Too often people invest for the next twelve months to three years. Most of the time people want to invest in what recently was a top performer. This I promise is a prescription for long term under performance and will end up costing you a lot sooner or later. Technology investing demonstrated this to many new investors in the late 1990s and early 2000s.

Let's start with a basic overview of the main investment types:

Bonds:

This is where you give money to a bank, company or individual and they pay you a fixed rate of interest per year over a fixed period of time. At the end of that time you get your original money back. This type of investing is low risk and low return. It is best suited for money that cannot be invested for the long term.

Always restrict your fixed income investments to both a short duration and to high quality. Bonds are typically purchased through a bond mutual fund. Banks offer Certificate of Deposits (CDs) that pay a fixed rate of return for fixed periods of time, 6 months, one year, or five years duration are common. An interest bearing checking account or money market account is really a bond type of investment but with no fixed term of investment.

Bank money market interest rates are usually lower than a mutual fund money market rate. Mutual fund bond funds with an average duration of around one year I still consider it to be a money market account, as the underlying value will be stable over most time periods, and the return should be much higher than a traditional money market account with a duration of only a week or at most one month. I consider the one year average duration bond fund an ideal place for money that you want quick access to but you are really not sure when you will need it. If you know you will need the money in the next few weeks then a bank money market fund will be acceptable.

Stocks:

When you own a stock you own a percentage of a company. Stocks typically have two aspects to their income, dividends and price. Dividends are usually paid semi annually. The price of stock changes daily. Stocks are liquid investments, meaning they can be converted to cash for a small transaction fee and a small spread between the buy and sell price. They are risky in the short run (0-5 years) they may or may not be reliable over the medium term (5-15 years). They produce reliably superior returns to bonds in the long run (15+ years).

In general you need an investment holding period of 7 years before investing in stocks. Stocks are considered risky. Stocks have a long history of yielding a higher return than bonds over the long term (15 years or more). Success in stock investing requires a long term hold, and diversification is typically found through mutual funds.

Real estate:

Real estate ownership is the most complex having a current income component (rent); a current cost (loan payment and maintenance costs) and the underlying real estate can appreciate or depreciate in price. Each holding of real estate is costly to purchase, difficult to convert to cash, and overall is considered a moderately risky investment.

Personal savings:

Most banks and brokerage houses offer a money market account that has no restrictions on additions or withdrawal and pays interest daily, at a relatively low rate. Term savings accounts have restrictions on withdrawal in exchange for paying a higher rate of interest.

Mutual funds offer a variety of fixed income investment alternatives. The most common type used by individual investors is money market funds and medium term bond funds. You can easily get your money out of a bond fund with no penalty. Bond funds have various durations in the underlying assets they hold. I prefer these over CDs or savings accounts with withdrawal restrictions.

You have to do your homework to understand what the bond fund invests in. You need to know the average maturity (duration) and the quality grade of the holdings (investment grade, corporate or junk). Make sure the duration of the bond fund you choose is five years or less and the quality of the bond fund is investment grade or corporate. Avoid junk bonds.

Brokerage accounts also offer money market and bond funds, but typically their fees are higher than a low cost provider like Vanguard.

IRA savings:
Mutual funds are your best choice for establishing a long term investment account like an IRA. I recommend Vanguard mutual funds and Vanguard IRA for several reasons.

Vanguard's IRA annual fees are some of the lowest in the industry and are eliminated once the IRA grows a little bit larger. These fees can really eat into your account growth when you are first starting out.

Vanguard's mutual funds have the lowest operating cost and turnover rate (rate at which assets in the fund are bought and sold) in the business. This means that your net earnings after fees and costs are better year after year with Vanguard.

Vanguard is one of the largest mutual fund families. This means they have just about every choice you really need for investing.

I do not recommend individual stock investing no matter how large your personal portfolio. It is just too hard to get good diversification from individual stock investments and it costs a lot more to trade and rebalance an individual stock portfolio. The data is clear that individual stock portfolios under perform low fee mutual funds over the long term, so why even bother?

Fees:

Perhaps one of the most important things to understand when you start investing in mutual funds is fees. Not all mutual funds are the same. In fact for essentially the same holdings different mutual funds will charge substantially different fees. These fund administration fees (operating fees) come right out of the return of the portfolio. Going with a mutual fund firm like Vanguard assures you that you are always paying one of the lowest possible fund administration fees for the type of fund you have chosen.

Loads:

Some mutual funds charge a load to invest or to sell. Typically these are not a good idea. They are a direct drag on your investment and studies show these funds actually under perform due to higher ongoing costs.

Firms like Schwab have "no load" mutual fund options. These funds charge a higher annual fund administration fee for Schwab to offer them to you in a convenient "no load" manner. These funds have a higher administration fee that acts like a hidden load and makes these a poor investment choice.

When a low cost provider like Vanguard has a back end or front end fee of 1 percent and they state this fee is only used to offset the cost of buying or selling, this fee is reasonable. Loads that go to advisors or an offering company like Schwab are avoidable, as they are really just sales loads.

What is the best fund to invest in today?

TV shows and investment magazines always market what is the best place or stock to put your money in today. This advice is preoccupied with what has been hot, not on how to invest today for the next fifteen years. This kind of advice is a prescription for under performance. It is a bubble based investing, more likely to produce large correction losses than large additional gains in the near future as they promise.

By the time everyone is talking about what is hot it has already done a major run up in price and the value has little room for growth or is headed for a substantial correction.

So how should you invest your hard earned savings to maximize its long term growth? Now you are asking the right question. It is the quality of our questions that determine our successes over time.

The first question you must address is how long is this money going to be invested for? If it is 7 years or less stay in bonds. Over 7 years consider stocks or real estate.

Next ask yourself what is the objective of my investment. If this is long term money for your retirement many years in the future then you need to seek an aggressive investment mix.

If you want to use this money for a down payment on a home within 10 years then you need mostly conservation of principal with some appreciation.

What if that home purchase will be i -5 years? Since the investment time horizon is less than 7 years it should be a short or medium term bond fund.

Individual stocks vs. mutual funds:

This is really a no-brainer; mutual funds are the way to go. Mutual funds can give you proper diversification even with a small initial investment. Investing in individual stocks is more akin to gambling and for the vast majority of investors it is inappropriate. You can start an IRA mutual fund with around $1,000 and add as little as $25 a month to the account. Individual stock investing is more like gambling than investing. This is taking you in the wrong direction with your decision making about investing.

Mutual funds:

I recommend index or asset class mutual funds. These are funds that invest in an entire asset class or a mathematically defined subset of an asset class.

The opposite of an index fund in an actively managed fund. Here the fund manager picks and chooses stocks for you over time.

The long term data is overwhelmingly in favor of index funds over actively managed funds. The seductive story that a particular manager can consistently out perform index funds is a powerful but ill-founded belief. The data consistently demonstrates over the long term this is a remote possibility. Using active management is letting someone else do your individual stock investing.

Diversification

In general this subject would take another book to do properly. I have done that in my book called *"Successful Investing"*. To learn more about this go to the following website. http://healthywealth.com/bookscdsdvds.php .

The remaining part of this chapter on investing is an introduction to investment diversification for risk control and return maximization.

Stocks / bonds / real estate

These are your three main investment asset classes; stocks, bonds and real estate.

Investment portfolios

Here are three sample portfolio mixes for a young adult investing in a long term IRA portfolio.

Aggressive mix
10% in bonds, 45% in stocks and 45% in real estate.

Normal mix
20% in bonds, 45% in stocks and 35% in real estate.

Conservative mix
40% in bonds, 40% in stocks and 20% in real estate.

Stocks:

Large stocks or small stocks.

All together there are about 9,000 U.S. individual stocks. The largest 500 of these make up more than two thirds the value of all stocks. The other 8,500 make up one third the value of stocks in the U.S. market and they are called small stocks. Large stocks are less volatile and more stable on the whole. Small stocks have a lot more risk and over a long time (20 years or more).

It is good to have both large and small stocks in your portfolio. A good rule of thumb for all investors is to have most of your stocks in large stocks. Never have more than 40% of your stocks in small stocks, they are just too risky. Having around 25% of your stocks in small stocks is an ideal percentage.

Putting one quarter to one half of your large stock allocation into real estate is a good diversification rule. Most investment professionals recommend 15 percent of the overall portfolio in real estate.

If 80% of the portfolio is in stocks and you put 25% of that in small stocks, and put 50% of the balance into real estate, the real estate portion of the overall portfolio turns out to be 30%. Thus, my rule runs from the typical recommendation to double that. The long term data supports that real estate is an excellent diversification strategy to stock investing, and that is the reason for my recommended that you hold a percentage of your investment in real estate. For more information see my book *Successful Investing* http://healthywealth.com/bookscdsdvds.php .

Value stocks or growth stocks.

A value stock is a stock whose price, divided by the accounting book value, is high. A growth stock is a stock whose price, divided by book value, is low. In 2004 eBay was a growth stock, and Sears was a value stock. Basically, the faster a company has been growing of late the more likely it is a growth stock. The more price correction a company has taken in the last few years the more likely it is now a value stock.

The data shows that depressed stocks (value stocks) on average going forward will outperform the average stock market by around 2 percent a year. Growth stocks on average going forward will under perform by around 1 percent a year.

When I recommend that you not invest more money in what just outperformed but instead put money into what just under-performed you might think I seem a little out of touch with things. In aggregate and over time this is what works.

There are periods of time when growth stocks do better than value stocks. Such was the case for several years in a row in the late 1990s. Because this does happen it is important to own some growth stocks as well as value stocks.

Small value stocks
25% of your U.S. stocks should be in small stocks. 100% of these should be in a small stock value index fund. Do not buy any growth stocks in this asset class. Do not buy a full index fund in this asset class. If you need more information and a better explanation for this I refer you to my book *"Successful Investing"*.

With large U.S. stocks, (75% of your U.S. stock investment), first split this allocation with real estate. I recommend between 25 to 50 percent of this allocation should go to real estate.

The large U.S. stock investment should be invested between value, growth and the full index. Here are three examples of how you might do that.
- ◆ 100% in an S&P 500 index fund.
- ◆ 50% in a S&P 500 index fund, and 50% in a large U.S. stock value index fund
- ◆ 60% in a large U.S. stock value index fund and 40% in a large U.S. stock growth fund (index or actively managed).

International stocks:
When you start out you can stay 100% in U.S. stocks. At some point you should start adding some international stocks for more diversification. You can bring the international portion of your stock portfolio up to 25%. The international stocks should be around

80% in large and 20% in small stocks.

Bonds:
Use a Vanguard investment grade (federal government treasuries or corporate high grade bonds) short duration (5 yr average maturity or less) bond mutual fund.

In a long term portfolio bonds should make up between 10 to 40 percent of your overall portfolio.

Real estate:
REITs are real estate investment trusts; they are mutual funds that invest in only real estate. They pay a high dividend rate. Dividends are like interest on bonds, as they are current income. They also fluctuate in price like a stock. A REIT invests in a variety of real estate, and as such diversifies your investment as to types of real estate and the region of real estate held.

I strongly prefer Vanguard for REIT investment. REIT investment fees vary substantially from one mutual fund family to another. Vanguard's REIT fees were considerably lower than all other REIT mutual funds in 2003, according to Morningstar.

Buying a house:
This subject is beyond the scope of the subject of this book but some of you may be interested in planning for this purchase so I have included a reference to an online article I wrote on this subject http://healthywealth.com/articles/home-purchase.pdf.

Chapter 14 - Gambling

Gambling is different than investing. It is important to understand the difference. Gambling is actually a disease. When you get hooked the disease owns your beliefs and actions.

Gambling provides you with an adreline rush. This is what you get addicted to. The rush comes from the recovery after a fall not just from winning. You cannot know how good it feels to win unless you know what it feels like to be in trouble. Getting yourself out of trouble and back in a healthy place is a powerful feeling. Unfortunately, to get the full rush again you need to get yourself back into the loss condition to feel the full rush of recovery. This is hard for someone else to be around.

Perhaps what you feel now when you gamble is nothing like what I just described. You may be in it for the feeling of winning not differentiating this from winning after losing. If so you might equate gambling to wanting a little incentive to succeed. You justify that having money on the line makes you focus and perform better. A lot of top athletes do this. At this stage gambling may not yet be an addiction. Like with smoking, it does not start out as an addiction but you cannot remember when it crossed the line, you just became addicted by continuing to do it regularly. At first you could stop anytime you wanted, but pretty soon you cannot.

The damaging thing about an addiction is that the addiction owns you, meaning it becomes more important than other things in your life. Others can see it in you yet you do not acknowledge the problem until you are deep into the addiction.

One way to understand how destructive gambling addiction can be is too see first hand what this disease can do to good people over time.

Go to an alcoholics' anonymous meeting and you will hear people share their desperate stories of gambling problems that went along with drinking. Read the local section of the Las Vegas newspaper and you will learn about the devastation that gambling creates in people's lives and to their families. Live near a gambling town and you will hear stories that will upset you. The dark side to gambling is not the crooks that run the game but the damage and unhappiness it creates in hard working honest people's lives.

There is only one way to be successful as a gambler: that is to own the gambling house.

When you bet with your friends on your performance you can consistently win as long as you are the top local competitor. Typically what happens however is you seek more challenging competition. This competition often plays for higher stakes. This new challenge can relieve you of several months winnings in a few days.

Another situation occurs where you take your competitive advantage and go from betting with friends on your performance to gambling in a new game. It does not take long for you to lose a lot of money fast.

Sooner or later even the best athletes go into a slump and finally loose their competitive advantage.

The sad part is the destruction from gambling is complete, predicable and inevitable. You have a choice, but the more regularly you gamble the harder it is to get out, just like any other addiction.

I have personally witnessed the destruction gambling can bring. The gambler once owned by the disease makes feeding the addiction the most important thing in his/her life. All other relationships get damaged as they get lowered in priority to gambling.

The addiction needs to hidden if it is to survive so several strategies of denial and protection are developed. All these hurt the people who are around the addict. The more successful the cloak to the addiction the more damage that is done. The defense can take many forms but basically the goal is to deflect criticism of the addiction and protect the control and access to funds to continue gambling. Distraction techniques are used to mask the fear of exposure. Clever life long gamblers have learned how to successfully keep the focus off themselves and keep it on others.

A cab driver told me a story of a friend of his whom at age 23 got a credit card with a ten thousand dollar limit. He flew to Las Vegas and lost the entire amount that weekend. He was already in debt and was hoping to hit it big and get out of all of his money problems. It did not work. He declared bankruptcy. A few months later his marriage ended. He was depressed and down and out for many years.

Another friend of his went to Las Vegas on occasion to play poker. He had a good job making about seventy thousand a year. He owned a large newer home in the suburbs. Over the last couple of years of occasional visits to Vegas he managed to max out his credit cards gambling. One Monday morning the cab driver got a call from a cop who said his friend was badly beaten up and needed sixty dollars for the bus trip back home. The cab driver agreed to help his friend out. A few months later this man had to sell his home to settle his Las Vegas debts.

A lot of gambling stories are kept in the dark. When you know these people personally over a long period of time you can see the destruction and havoc it creates in their life. From the outside it is hard to understand why they keep gambling when we all know that over time they are going to lose more than they win.

Another name for gambling should be the "Value Distruction Disease". The destruction is not just to money but also to relationships and the self esteem of the people assocaited with the gambler. Gambling is like smoking, do it repeatedly and you will become an addict. Do it occasionally and and it might just be entertainment. As soon as you find yourself consumed with thoughts of betting you have become an addict. If you ignore the warning signs you could end up having it run your actions and cause great harm to your relationships. Gambling is something you must be very cautious with, as the destruction it can bring to your life can be complete.

Chapter 15 - Self Sufficiency

Financial support comes at a price. Often the price is your self worth. Self worth is how you feel about yourself. Your happiness is in large part dependent on how you feel about yourself?

Getting more "stuff" does not raise your self worth. We all know someone whose family is well off and provided them an expensive car and nice things and yet they feel insecure inside.

Financial help has the potential to raise self esteem but most of the time it does the opposite. Financial help from your parents often lowers your self esteem.

Any financial help from a loving parent we assume to be well intended, and therefore must be good, right? Most of the time, in today's world, financial help from the family is more harmful than helpful because of how it is given.

Have your ever felt resentful of the financial help you have received either because of the strings attached or because you resented some part of how it was given? Have you ever felt undeserving or troubled by receiving gifts or financial help?

Receiving something without a fair exchange leaves the receiver with a loss of self worth. The giver feels good. It may not show up the first or the second time but over a long time the receiver knows he or she is not feeling good about things, and often blames these feelings on the giver being too controlling.

The problem is created because these gifts were given as an incomplete exchange. The receiver has actually suffered a loss of self worth for unfairly receiving. It is so subtle and common place that you are not even aware of what actually happened. Let's look at an extreme example to understand my point.

You just tuned 16 and you ask for and received a brand new luxury car. Of course it is the color you wanted. You have not been required to get a job to pay for gas or insurance or anything like that. Is this an ideal situation? Or is this a curse? Unfortunately this is a serious problem for the 16 year old, yet it seems like everything she was wishing for.

There is an easy solution to have this be a benefit rather than a curse, there needs to be an exchange. The gift also needs to be age appropriate (what you could afford to do for yourself at this age if working full time).

I have found two things are needed to create exchange in this situation:

First, you need a set of written rules that govern the car acquisition process. Second, you need to do all the tasks asked of you by the rules. The essence of your contribution is that you will do the research, you will provide written documentation showing conformation to the rules and finally and you will negotiate the deal.

Here are my general rules for parental support in a car purchase for a young adult:
♦　　You must work and save $500 (or $x,xxx) towards the purchase of the car.
♦　　The maximum purchase price will be $xx,xxx, before sales tax, and registration fees.
♦　　The car make, model and year must be on the recommended car list by consumer reports (new car list for a new car, used car list for a used car). Printout required to prove it.
♦　　The car being considered must get at least 20 miles per gallon city mileage according to the EPA numbers for that make, model and year. Printout required to prove it.
♦　　The insurance costs must be no more than 25% greater than a same year model Honda Accord LX, and a written quote must be obtained from an insurance company to prove this before the purchase of this model is approved.
♦　　The car must be no more than 4 years old, if you are going to use it for college, 6 years if just for high school.
♦　　It must have less than 60,000 miles if you are going to use this car through college, 80,000 if just for high school.
♦　　A Kelly blue book printout is required before you can go

shopping and your parents can set a purchase price you cannot exceed.

♦ New cars require a Consumer Report's New Car Report on the final model you are shopping for to help your parents set you a price limit.

♦ New car purchase limit is based on dealer invoice price plus or minus some amount set by your parent.

♦ Used car price limit is based on Kelly Blue Book Trade-in value plus some amount set by the parent. You must print this out with all the features on the car you are considering.

♦ You (the young adult) must negotiate the purchase of the car. Your parents will set a dollar limit on what you can negotiate with the seller or the car sales person. If you are under 18 your parents must sign the deal for it to be legally binding. You can negotiate, but the salesperson knows your parents must sign. You will likely get treated with little respect, but that is how most car sales people treat all customers. Welcome to the uncomfortable process of buying a car. It is part of the process to learn to cope with this stress and still get what you want.

I had my kids do their own deals. I coached them and of course set the bargaining limits after they did the research. They each took with them either a friend or their sibling. Only one of the three got a deal on his/her first trip. All of them felt really empowered after it was all over. Their friends were amazed that they did the actual negotiating and got such a good deal.

Can you see the exchange in this program? Can you see a difference in your self reliance in this program? How about in your self worth? How dramatic is the difference in what you get out of these two approaches?

When one of your parents does something for you that you could do for yourself your parent creates dependency.

When dependent relationships continue into early adult life your self esteem and self reliance are lowered. I call this *The Entitlement Trap®*. If you are capable of negotiating for the purchase of a car with some parameters, what else are you capable of? I think lots more. In fact not letting you do more on your own is what is lowering your self esteem, reducing your happiness and damaging your self reliance. The trade off for your parents is the illusion that the control they still have is for your own good. Once you are in college it is not for your own good, instead it is for their control. It is difficult for most parents to make this transition. But until you are really independent you will not become self reliant, and without that how can you truly be happy with yourself?

How long can this go on? It can actually go on for the rest of your life. You can be a dependent of your parents until you die. It is in my opinion a curse, more like a prison of spirit than a silver spoon that makes life better. Having more things you did not earn does not make you happier. Expressing your inner gift to its fullest with love creates happiness.

The good news is *The Entitlement Trap®* takes two parties. Thus, either party can opt out. It is easier for the parent to stop the cycle, but you can also end the cycle. Make no mistake this is very hard to do. It is as difficult as quitting smoking after a long addiction. The problem is that these are your parents, people you love and who believe the control they are continuing is for your own good. They do not know that how they are going about influencing you is keeping you dependent on them and this is sustaining the problem. This condition is not well understood. Those who find themselves in this situation know they fell trapped, but do not understand what to do as they have been conditioned for a long time to relate with their parents in this way. Your odds of success increase when you understand the problem, and value a different outcome enough to change no matter what it cost. Your parents may still keep doing what they always did in trying to control you and shelter you from responsibility. You have the power to give yourself the gift of self reliance and high self worth.

Giving up financial support in order to be increase your self worth and happiness seems counter intuitive. For without the financial support your chances to make something of yourself are far less certain. How can accepting more responsibility by agreeing to more rules be anything but more control thus taking away more self esteem? Often that is the paradox we find in life and why the answer can be so close yet so hard to see? Going for self reliance is very scary and difficult only at first. There is no greater payoff in the end than giving yourself freedom, empowerment and the gift of self reliance. If you were to stand there near the end of your life and answer the question what would I have done differently, those with cursed with The Entitlement Trap would likely answer I should have chosen to learn early on in my life to make it myself before I ever received an inheritance or significant ongoing support.

Last year in Maui I met a young lady (about 28 years old) who came from a wealthy family in Europe. The family stands ready to help her get into one of the family businesses and enjoy a privileged life. She is young and beautiful which can make matters worse. The family also is ready to help her find the right partner. She instead decided to explore life in the U.S. and learn to make it on her own for a few years to figure out what she wanted to do in life. I applaud the courage it takes to do this and not expect any family financial help. If in the back of her mind she is just marking time until she gets family help this time apart will not work, it will just cement in the dependency. I get however, that she wants to learn to make it on her own. She met a lady while in Maui that owns several restaurants in the North East of the U.S. mainland. Last summer she left Maui to train in one of her restaurants. The goal was to first learn to manage a restaurants and then come back to Maui in a few years and help this lady open a restaurant that she gets a piece of the ownership in. There is no greater gift to the well being of a person that the self worth that comes from self reliance.

"Families and Money – The Entitlement Trap" is the title of my next book. You can check my website at http://HealthyWealth.com/bookscdsdvds.php to see when it will be published. You can also send me an email asking to be notified when it comes out from this website.

"Every dollar you earn is worth ten given to you. Earned money creates the self-image of self-reliance; given money creates the self-image of other-dependence."

– Tom Hopkins

To order more books

Money Basics for Young Adults

http://HealthyWealth.com/bookscdsdvds.php

http://Amazon.com

Money Basics for Young Adults - **PDF**

a pdf document is available at:

http://HealthyWealth.com/bookscdsdvds.php